THE LIME GREEN PLASTIC COVERED COUCH

INSIGHT FOR WOMEN WHO STRUGGLE TO FIND LASTING LOVE

Marion Baker, RTC

Produced by:

FriesenPress

Suite 300 – 852 Fort Street

Victoria, BC, Canada V8W 1H8

www.friesenpress.com

Distributed to the trade by The Ingram Book Company

The anecdotes in this book are used to illustrate common issues and problems that I have encountered and do not necessarily portray specific people or situations. No real names have been used where personal information is divulged.

As with all books, this one contains opinions and ideas of the author. It is intended to provide helpful and informative material on the subjects addressed in the publication. It is sold with the understanding that the author and publisher are not engaged in rendering psychological or any other kind of personal professional services or therapy in the book. The reader should consult his or her own psychological professional before adopting any of the concepts in this book or drawing inferences from it. The content of this book is general, whereas each reader's situation is unique. Therefore, as with all books of this nature, the purpose is to provide general information rather than address individual situations. The author and publisher specifically disclaim all responsibility for any liability, loss, or risk, personal or otherwise, which is incurred as a consequence, directly or indirectly, of the use and application of any of the contents of this book.

Baker takes a subject near and dear to our hearts and puts a new spin on an age old dilemma. How do we dance with the mystery of love and not get caught up in the fairy-tale fantasies of our youth? She approaches her own, and others' foibles in love, with such humor, humility, and warmth, that she draws us into their stories. Baker then takes things up a notch to a trans personal level. She offers us an understanding of why we do some of the crazy things we do to seek love, followed up with ideas on how to regain our sanity! She does a brilliant job of opening our minds, our eyes, and our hearts to examine our own role and responsibility in co-creating Real relationships. The Lime Green Plastic Covered Couch is an illuminating guide on the path to surrendering our illusions, and flowing into new steps in the dance of conscious partnership.

Denise Cunningham
Author of Whispers of Hope: Transcending Abuse,
Cancer and Divorce to Embrace Peace

Marion has taken a leap of faith and courage to share one of life's most elusive prizes: true love. It is often hidden in unrealistic fairy tales and expectations, unrequited love and pure fantasy. True love is truly about putting your own personal interests aside in support of the one you love, with this caveat: the love of your life will risk all and sacrifice all to express his affection and admiration for the woman in his life. It is not about being placed on a pedestal. It is about seeking equity with a peer who is your most trusted confidante, friend and lover. And to discover this beautiful Truth, there is a path of hurt and pain and the willingness to keep risking for love because it's worth it. Thanks Marion for bringing together these stories to help women share their collective experiences for the empowerment and support of all.

July Ono
President, On The Beach Education Corporation.

The Lime Green Plastic Covered Couch is a brilliant tool for women who want to more deeply connect to their inner wisdom using the mirror of relationship. It is essential reading for any woman struggling to attract, establish or maintain a conscious, loving, healthy relationship with a man and finding herself disappointed and broken-hearted. Based on her own struggles and ultimate success as well as those of others, Marion's book is filled with compassionate stories, shared with a sense of humour that will provide insight and clarity for transforming and deepening your relationship to yourself and Spirit/Universe so that you manifest the loving relationship that you deserve.

Ellen Hayakawa
Co-author of Healing the Heart of the World,
author of the Inspired Organization

TABLE OF CONTENTS

ACKNOWLEDGEMENTS

Bunny. (My husband Eddie) I can't tell you how many ways you support and inspire me. I learn a lot from your no non-sense way of seeing things and your ongoing love and kindness. Your solidity gives me something to springboard off of.

My best friend Liz. This book is so much better because of you. If we didn't work out all of this "man stuff" together, many of my blind spots would still be intact. And I'd probably still be single.

Duane and Catherine O'Kane. The world is a much better place because of the strong stand you make in it. I learned to love because of you; and I mean love in a profound way that has turned my life upside down and changed everything I thought was important.

Michele Hall, my book coach. Holy cow, there are no words. This book went from scribbles on a page to a work that I am proud of and one that I know we both hope will help many, many women.

Satu. A big thank you for all the times you were there for me when I struggled. You are a rock, my friend.

Karen. Your huge heart, your marketing and business experience and your entrepreneurial spirit kept me energized in the times I needed it most.

Scott Paton, my web designer and internet marketer. Your passion for what you do is brilliant. And your generous heart has inspired and helped me in so many ways, both personal and professional.

My Practitioners Training classmates. My second family. Thank you for holding my hand as we struggled together to learn to be bigger than we ever thought we could be. I will never forget you.

My Clearmind community. My peeps. You are the continued inspiration that helps me to know who I am and inspires me to keep giving. I love all of you.

My blood family. My Mom and my sisters. Last but definitely not least. Thank you for being such down to earth, solid people. I love you and I really appreciate having you in my life.

FOREWORD

Marion Baker is intense and committed to whatever she does. Through the course of her life these qualities have resulted in an interesting mix of being both a blessing and a curse. Such is the case for all of us this, our best strengths also carry the potential to be our worst weaknesses. All of us carry on an ongoing debate inside ourselves about how we make use of our go-to default tools in our tool kit. What shall we use it for – to heal or to harm? Marion has clearly made the choice to heal, and articulates a path for others to follow in this book.

Marion's style will become obvious to anyone reading this book or spending time with her. Marion throws caution to the wind in her life, and her ambition and adventurous spirit is present in these written words as well. The Lime Green Plastic Covered Couch is consistent with the way she lives her life. If her life had theme song, Marion's would be "Set your controls for the heart of the Sun." The heart of life is the only place to go, and it is the only place she is interested in.

Marion has taken this opportunity to share the wisdom of her journey, to open up the profound learning and healing that is available in the middle of inevitable personal crisis.

Marion articulates her understanding with a passionate and intelligent delivery.

We have always been impressed with Marion's humility and heart-centredness. Marion has been part of our company, Clearmind International Institute Inc., since 2002. Her contributions to our company and vision have been invaluable. Whenever we question a decision or discuss a direction that we might take, we only have to look across the room at our heart barometer Marion to gauge if we are on a proper course or not. If Marion produces a tear we know we can trust where we are heading because we know we have come from our heart.

Put the kettle on, put your feet up, open this book and spend some time with the heart of Marion Baker. She will touch yours, and open you up to a new way of being.

Duane and Catherine O'Kane

PÏECES OF THE PUZZLE

I remember a moment as a little girl when my Mom was mad and yelling at me. I stood transfixed as she turned into a crazed demon. Her eyes glowed red and her face twisted in a rage that I didn't understand. I had no idea what I had done wrong and I felt terrified and guilty. My family life was ruled by many such moments and yet my heart kept insisting, "No, this isn't the way it should be. I don't like feeling guilty all the time. I don't know why life is like this, but I know there's a better way and I want to find it."

Fast-forward thirty years. I was hired to cook for Clearmind International at their Retreat Centre with no idea who they were and what they were about. I had no intention of taking any of their personal development courses as I had become disillusioned by years of workshops. I had never found the significant changes that these courses always promised. As far as I was concerned, someone got richer while I didn't get any happier. I definitely hadn't found my little girl's dream of a better way to live.

I had been working at the retreat centre for three years when one day I felt someone walk into the kitchen behind me. I turned to see a woman almost gliding across the floor as if she were walking on a cloud. I was taken aback.

I had met her three years earlier when she first enrolled in the Clearmind training program. She had seemed needy, pathetic and someone to avoid if at all possible. Now she stood before me, strong, confident, alive and comfortable in her own skin with such calm, loving presence that I instantly felt compelled to get to know her. What's more, I wanted to be like that myself.

I took a second look at the other three-year graduates. It was clear they had all had similar personal transformations. What had created such dramatic shifts? Finally, this seemed to be what I had been searching for.

I began what I consider my greatest personal achievement – a three-year journey that completely transformed my life and finally met the needs of a little girl who wanted to be loved.

My teachers showed me where and how I have stunted my emotional growth. Anita Moorjani describes this beautifully in her book, *Dying To Be Me*. She says it's like there's a brilliant white light (our source), which we filter through a prism (our human ego), then all the colours split off in different directions (our feelings). Some of them feel uncomfortable, so we cut off that colour and push it down so we don't have to ever feel it again. We are left not expressing the whole brilliance of the white light, just the parts of it we judge to be acceptable.

I noticed for myself that as I cut off the colours that I didn't want to feel, the remaining colours dulled as well. My emotions had a very narrow spectrum and couldn't shine in all the hues that are available. What I used to call love turned out to be a very watered down version of what is possible once I was not afraid to allow the full rainbow of feelings.

Before taking Clearminds three-year counsellor training program I didn't know what it was like to have a lasting relationship with a man or to be a true, supportive friend or what it was like to feel love for my parents. My Mom had always been the Big Bad Ogre. It's impossible to have a meaningful relationship with that picture in mind. I now see her as a sweet little old lady who reacts with big emotions when she feels threatened. My perception of her changed when I came to realize that her critique came with good intent, so I was finally able to tell her lovingly that her criticism was no longer okay. I created my own sense of safety. Knowing that I cannot be hurt, I can reach out with kindness now, rather than fight her.

After going through three intense years with my classmates, I have a group of very close friends who are all counsellors. Whenever I need help they provide strong and loving support. And I live a more fulfilled and inspired life when I get to flex my newfound friendship muscles and contribute to their lives.

Best of all, after years of short-term serial monogamous relationships I am now married to a fabulous guy who loves me and meets my desire to build a happy relationship. I have learned to be the kind of person who stays when the going gets tough rather than one who runs at the first sign of trouble. I have come to realize that the difficulties in life were, in fact, not other people or difficult situations but my own ego-based machinations. The Clearmind community has been the inspiration and support of my inner transformation and that change has turned my life around by one hundred and eighty degrees. I finally found the loving appreciation I had been searching for as a little girl and I discovered the access to it was through developing the relationships I had in my life. Forgiveness was the key that unlocked it all.

There's a reason this book has landed in your hands. You, too, are looking for a new world where love lives and thrives.

It is possible. I found it and I'd like to share my journey and the journey of others who also didn't know what was getting in their way.

We can't create a world of kindness, love and appreciation alone. If we're going to live in the way that we know in our hearts is possible, there have to be others willing to join hands to do it together. Our relationships become opportunities to connect with our own inner source and wisdom and the world opens up to possibilities we didn't know existed.

Thank you, Duane and Catherine for opening up this new perspective for many others and for me. This world is a much better place because of your determination, your persistent caring and your heart.

THE LIME GREEN PLASTIC COVERED COUCH

Insight For Women Who Struggle
To Find Lasting Love

Introducing the cast:

I thought I was having one of the best happy-to-be-alive moments, when the Universe knocked on my door to make it even juicier. I was snuggled in with my delicious new husband, Eddie, on our lime green plastic covered couch, decked out in fuzzy slippers and my favourite save-the-drama-for-the-llama flannel pyjamas. The smell of freshly made popcorn lingered in the air and we were settled in on a rainy night to watch a great old movie rerun on TV. With a click of the remote, the movie came alive and we got ready to lose ourselves in other people's lives for the evening.

The next thing Eddie knew I was dancing around the living room, popcorn flying, and slippers somersaulting through the air. "Bunny! Bunny!" I yelled (we call each other Bunny), "That's it! What that woman just said is the whole point of my book! She gets it!"

Opening scene:

Irene, a dowdy pre-pubescent teen, is a chauffeur's daughter who constantly ogles the two rich sons of her father's employer. Naturally, Irene doesn't have a crush on the reliable stable one. She has a crush on the freewheeling, irresponsible, handsome playboy brother. Since she is just the hired help, she only gets to dream from afar and never really gets to interact with the boys. They're also few years older and for them she is simply invisible.

Cut to scene eight years later:

Irene has blossomed into a beautiful young woman. Her father thinks it wise to send her to France to work for a year so she can become more independent and cultured.

Cut to exterior café in Paris. The Eiffel Tower looms in the distance.

Irene and her boss, Yvonne, a lovely cultured French woman, are having a casual chat while sipping espresso. Irene is talking about a man at work who has asked her out.

Irene: He's nice, but my heart is elsewhere.

Yvonne: Is that the fellow you've mentioned casually forty or fifty times since you arrived?

Irene: He keeps me company.

Yvonne: It sounds as though you're in love with an illusion. Illusions are dangerous people. They have no flaws.

Well knock me over and call me Susan! That sums up this book in a nutshell.

If Irene's story has started to ring some bells but you're not quite sure if this book is for you, then let me help you decide. This book is for you if you have struggled to find or keep relationships and if you continually find yourself disappointed and broken-hearted, even while in one. You will hear stories from many women who struggle to keep love in their lives. The intention of the stories is to open your eyes to what is preventing you from being happy in a relationship.

I know it's fun to slip off your sensible Mary Janes for a moment to daydream yourself into the stilettos of friends who regale you with stories of their latest date or conquest. The femme fatale who is happy dating or seeing someone casually and who says, "And then he poured Champagne down my cleavage and you can just GUESS what happened next!" This book wasn't written for them. This book was written for women who are looking to find lasting love, yet struggle to make it happen.

My intention is that these stories will spark insightful inquiries so that you can walk your own path to love and lessen the gap between fantasy and reality. In that way you can dance along to a healthier and happier way of life. Be aware that this may involve a sudden left turn from the road you are now on. You will learn to ask for help, become open to receiving it, learn to connect with others and come to understand the value of exposing yourself, bumps, warts and all. Sometimes the help may need to come from a professional counsellor; sometimes it may come in the form of asking your friend or partner just to sit and hold your hand while you cry.

With a little insight, vulnerability and the realization that we can make different choices at any moment, any relationship can be transformed. I will debunk the myth about all your problems being the fault of the guy in your life. Instead, we will examine why you choose the men you do and then go on to react to them the way you do. The tools in this book can help you make better choices about who to get into bed with, so to speak.

What you may surmise as you read is that the women who share these stories are incapable of leading effective lives. They must be simpering wallflowers with whom you would have nothing in common as all they do is sit around and do nothing but whine. Yet, nothing is further from the truth. The women featured in these pages are strong, independent entrepreneurs, successful career women, great mothers, fully functioning human beings whose Achilles heel happens to be intimate male/female relationships.

As you read, you will find I am a big advocate of counselling, especially Transpersonal therapy, which I'll explain more about as we go along. I would encourage everyone (yes, everyone – unless you can already walk on water and turn water into wine) to find a good counsellor at the tough points in life. Not only can they help you navigate the rough waters of personal crises, they can help you evolve beyond your struggles in ways you never imagined.

Here's your first tip: keep an open mind. If you find yourself resistant, or saying to yourself, "That's not me at all" or "I would never do that!" then pause. Any reaction is an indication that you may have a blind spot. So instead of shutting down, remain curious. The only way to change the results you are getting is to try something new, so here's your chance to see if you, too, have been in love with an illusion.

The Cast of Characters

There will be a few voices along the road that you may find helpful. Since I look at things from a counsellor's perspective, I will occasionally insert a comment from **Counselling Mind**. **Counselling Mind** has an outside perspective and offers a fresh viewpoint, while also having a great deal of empathy. **Counselling Mind** is the one you call after you show up unannounced on the doorstep of your new man's house in your sexy new hot pink dress with a bottle of his favorite red. But you're the one who gets surprised when you hear the titter of another woman's laughter from upstairs as he opens the door wearing, well...not much.

Other times you will come across fight or flight **Lizard Brain**. He shows up a little more often than I would like. Imagine a gecko running away at full speed with its arms in the air, screaming, "Run away, danger, danger!" He's an impulsive character. He knows when it's time to run away from something that really isn't going in the direction you're looking for. He is also the one who can keep you stuck by running away from what he sees as trouble when it isn't always. Sometimes he wins and sometimes **Counselling Mind** adds some much needed discernment, as Lizard Brain is rather flighty.

You will meet a few other characters: **Pollyanna, Florence Nightingale** and the **Wicked Witch of the West**. Most importantly you will meet **Cinderella** who has wonderful, big dreams and a beautiful, romantic vision of life. This quality is her greatest gift and her arch nemesis. Cinderella gets caught in a fantasy world that can never come true and that leaves her pining and heart-broken. She thinks her dreams will become reality just by magic and that the man of her dreams will really, truly ride up on his white steed to rescue her. He will meet her every need and whim without her ever having to ask. And life will never change from the blissful, head over heels in love stage.

Alison Pearson, the author of *I Think I Love You,* says, "The teen idol crush is really, really powerful. It's a dress rehearsal for love. You're in love with the Idea of being in love."

It's when we get stuck at this stage that it becomes the **Cinderella Fantasy**, which, if you look at the staggering divorce rate, should be considered a cultural epidemic. Many women in these pages are caught up in **Cinderella's Fantasy**, including me, and if you are reading this book, likely you too. Many of us are in the same boat. The question is – how do we jump into the water and learn to swim without drowning?

The journey that culminated in writing this book was a long, tear-filled struggle that at the same time was also filled with joyful, fun and illuminating moments. At forty-eight years old, I finally found love and marriage. And yet, despite the joys of living with a delicious man, it was still not the happily-ever-after ending I grew up believing was my destiny. Instead, what I discovered is that a successful relationship requires ongoing, everyday choices about what kind of partner I wish to be.

Let me begin with my own story. True to my character, I will be brutally honest about it as I tell you how I learned to doggie paddle after I got tired of being at sea all alone, then finally held my nose and jumped out of the boat.

THE LIME GREEN PLASTIC COVERED COUCH

CHAPTER 1

When Prince Charming Falls Off His Horse

The tops of the old-growth trees swayed in the wind as we drove down the windy road in our trusty white steed (Eddie's convertible Mustang – and yes, it's white). I caught the scent of cedar and my heart leapt like a kid at Christmas as we arrived at the Wickaninnish Inn, an exclusive retreat that had been on my bucket list for years.

Our room overlooked the beach so we could watch the wild ocean waves crash on the shore while we lounged warmly in a huge soaker tub for two. We had bought the Elopement Package and all we had to do was show up; every detail taken care of. It was a beautiful September day and I was here to marry an old flame who had held a candle for me for more than two decades.

Eddie wore a stunning, off-white suit with a black shirt and man jewellery, which I love. His bracelets and necklaces were iconic of the free spirits we are. I wore a gorgeous, knee-length, flowing halter dress, with tiny white flowers in my long, dark, curly hair and open sandals that tied up my calf. I would have preferred bare feet, but a girl can't be too careful when wandering around the wilderness of Vancouver Island.

A small group gathered at the beach, the sun on our backs and the play of the surf keeping time with our vows. My dress and hair were blowing in the breeze off the ocean.

Eddie's firm, deep voice carried above the wind: "Marion, you are my one true love. I have spent a lifetime looking for a girl like you."

Sigh.

The female minister and witness stood there, mouths open, glassy eyed, speechless, completely captivated by the moment.

As we kissed, the photographer proclaimed, "That was one of the *best* kisses I've ever seen, and I've seen hundreds of kisses."

We laughed and kissed our way through our photos. We played in the surf, snuggled on benches beneath huge cedar trees and giggled as we walked through the long grasses that bordered the beach.

We talked and laughed through a slow dinner, sipping Champagne and watching the setting sun as it painted the sky in reds and oranges. Unable to take our eyes off each other, we stretched the moments to try to make them last forever.

We finally got the hint from our sleepy-eyed waiters and headed back to our room to discover dozens of tea lights flickering a warm glow and the gentle scent of rose petals scattered across the bed. The soaker tub overflowed with bubbles and more rose petals, while yet another bottle of Champagne stood in a bucket of ice by the bed accompanied by a gorgeous chocolate mousse cake. I thought I had died and gone to heaven.

I was never one to dream about a big church wedding. The idea of a white cream-puff dress and bridesmaids all decked out like Christmas tree ornaments with two hundred ancient uncles I've never met drooling over me for a kiss didn't exactly sound enticing. As a forty-eight-year-old bride, a private wedding on the beach was beyond my wildest dreams.

When I first met Eddie, I was a cocky, young twenty-six-year-old in short skirts and high heels, with a wink and a smile for all the boys. Eddie was nineteen, a cute young cub in tight jeans and dirty blond hair – a charming combo of sweet and masculine.

I wasn't serious about anything at that age. I was the consummate free spirit, constantly socializing and hobnobbing. I was out to have lots of fun with whoever wanted to come along for the ride. I was definitely not ready to settle down for marriage and babies.

We met as co-workers at a large, local electronics and music chain and dated for just over a year. As the older woman, I opened his eyes to the ways of the world with mixed reactions from him. I fed him sushi, he spat it out. I took him camping. He hated it. He tolerated facial masks and cucumbers on his eyes only because he loved my zest for life. Our relationship ended when I went away with my girlfriends and had a brief holiday fling.

What I didn't realize at the time was that he was devastated. He had been madly in love with a girl who had no concept of what love was. I had no idea how much I had hurt him.

Twenty-two years later he showed up on Facebook and suggested we get together for old time's sake. He drove up in his white steed, top down, and took me to a beach where we wandered and talked for hours. Memories rushed back and with a jolt of recognition, I realized Eddie was the guy I had been searching for all along. I had fun with him, I could count on him, I felt safe with him, I felt as though he considered my best interests, and furthermore I was very attracted to him. It had taken me all these years to figure out what I wanted and here he was, a dashing, bemused apparition from my past.

What I thought would be a casual lunch turned into a confessional as Eddie shared the pain he had felt so many years ago. "I was so madly in love with you. You are the only woman I ever cried over. I kept wondering how I could have been different so that you would stay."

My heart melted. It reminded me of Jack Nicholson's drop-dead line to Helen Hunt in the movie *As Good As It Gets*, "You make me want to be a better man."

Sigh.

Eddie said, "I knew I would have to grow up, which is why I called you ten years later."

"You what?"

"You turned me down. Nicely, but with no explanation."

I could remember neither the phone call nor my rejection of him.

"After holding out hope for more than a decade, I gave up. I had been looking for another girl just like you, but never found one."

More sighing and heart melting.

This time though, I was sold. Sparks flew like wildfire. We met up again in July and were married the following September. I can almost hear millions of computers being booted up as women rush to Facebook to look up their old flames.

A few dates into our new relationship, Eddie kept telling me he would marry me in a heartbeat, but I still needed a bit more time.

We were now spending all our time together and had planned to go away the following weekend. We were chatting about possible destinations while shopping in a funky Vancouver neighbourhood when I stopped dead in my tracks in front of a jewellery store. I was staring at the ring I had always pictured I would be married with. It was very artsy and very specific, and there it was, winking at me from inside the display case.

"There's my ring!" I shouted in excitement. If this had been a popcorn and fuzzy slippers moment, there would have been a cacophony of things flying in the air. Without a moment's hesitation, Eddie walked in, bought the ring and proposed to me right there on the street.

For thirty years I had been through the gamut of screening hundreds of men, primarily on the Internet. I discovered, mostly the hard way, how to check in with myself and to trust my instincts. Now as Eddie nervously waited, sweat starting to bead up on his brow, I asked myself one last time: "Does this feel right?" "Does this feel like my next step?" I got a resounding, "Yes!" In that moment the clouds parted, the angels sang and I was finally ready to take the plunge.

Our plans for the next weekend were now sealed. At a moment's notice, we were off to the Wickaninnish Inn.

If you're not sighing and your heart isn't melting, perhaps you have been hurt too many times and have grown cynical about love and marriage. Happily ever after does include some bumps and detours along the way.

Post-Wedding Day Reality –
Where The Heck Did I Put My Tiara?

Case in point. Let's check in with Cinderella and Prince Charming, five years into happily ever after.

Cinderella cringes as she hears her eight-month-old twins, bellies empty, diapers full, screaming at the top of their lungs. "Phew! What did I feed them that would smell like that?" She looks at the pile of diapers in the corner waiting to be washed and the clean diaper drawer is...empty! The last of the formula was gone at three in the morning.

The three-year-old is calling, "Mommy, Mommy, I did it all by myself."

She looks out of the window to spot a large hole dug into the garden where the prized petunias used to be and where her triumphant three-year-old now stands, covered in mud from head to toe.

The Prince, now balding and beer-bellied, belches as he sits on the couch watching the game. "Hey honey, what's for dinner tonight? I was thinking I'd invite the boys over!"

And, then, if she gets the least bit upset, she gets the stink-eye stare from Prince Charming with the what-happened-to-the-sweet-girl-I-married guilt trip.

Ahhhh, wedded bliss! Ain't it grand?

This is definitely a scene that would have ended up on the cutting room floor and one that would have us all running away from marriage faster than you can say Fairy God Mother.

Now, if you're expecting to hear stories about how shortly after my honeymoon ended that Eddie turned into a balding, belching, beer-bellied, demanding husband, you will be disappointed. My husband is kind and he loves me deeply. I am glad I chose him. Nonetheless, be prepared to have your bubble burst as you learn the reality of living with Prince Charming after the wedding.

For Eddie, cleaning is not necessary. Shortly after moving in with him I phoned to tell him proudly that I had scrubbed the bathroom. "Why?" he asked, completely dumbfounded.

Our couch is wrapped in heavy, lime green plastic following a rumour that a neighbour down the hall had bedbugs. Our bed is still in its original plastic packaging for the same reason.

Eddie is very practical. He knows that Rubbermaid tubs make great furniture: tables, cat beds and footstools, all handily filled with things that might be useful one day. He has so many of these handy dandy tubs that you have to crab-walk sideways down the hallway to enter the apartment.

Being a die-hard sports fan, he collects and proudly displays all things sporty: sports jerseys, sports lighters, sports mugs, sports blankets and sports pillow cases. The female equivalent would be an apartment decorated in white eyelet lace, pink slipcovers on the furniture, fuzzy pillows and Hello Kitty paraphernalia gracing every corner.

"Never throw something away if you can pile it on top of something else you don't want to throw away" is Eddie's motto because you never know when you're going to need it. Consequently, the balcony is littered with odd bits of carpet, old bathmats, Astroturf, rotting plants and other valuable things that should never, ever be thrown away.

Because he fears the cat will fall or jump through the railings, he has fenced off a three by four foot section for the cat to move around in. Sadly, anyone else who goes onto the balcony also gets stuck in kitty cat jail.

Eddie thinks this place has lots of character and he refuses to move. In my eyes the apartment is an outdated, ugly dump. In addition to bed-bug guy down the hall, there are the drug dealers, Chester and Chico, two doors down and Mac on the first floor who yells at imaginary people and will punch you if you catch him on the wrong day. Our surly landlord, Gilles, wanders around in a sweaty, tight white undershirt with way too hair much exploding out of it.

What about dining out with Prince Charming? Sandwiches, burgers, hot dogs, Kraft Dinner, pizza, donuts, chocolate bars, and popular brands of kiddies' sugary cereal that come with a surprise in every box are Eddie's idea of haute cuisine. Ordering Chinese is a long-lost luxury, as is my favourite, Tandoori chicken. An evening on the town is now deciding which pub or burger joint has a two-for-one deal. My high heels and dresses are gathering dust in the back of my closet.

Remember I mentioned we were free spirits? It turns out, I'm the free spirit – Eddie is not. I'm ready at the drop of a hat to throw on a backpack or get on a plane to head for a destination well off the beaten path. Eddie refuses to even entertain the concept of an all-inclusive Mexican resort. He knows there's a bandit lurking around every corner waiting to steal his wallet and that Montezuma will be swift with his revenge if he ventures from the tried and true. No doubt about it, tropical places have too many things that can kill you. Even pitching a tent at the local lake is out of the question. Too many bugs! On occasion, he will give in to my wanderlust as long as it's a pre-booked five-star vacation where we don't stray too far outside Eddie's personally defined safety criteria.

Okay, now I can hear many of you thinking, "Oh my God! How can she live like that! Not only is he crazy but she's obviously insane to stand for that."

Not too many years ago I would have agreed. Like other single women who haven't yet found the right guy, my **Lizard Brain** would have grabbed its backpack and run screaming to Tahiti.

Long-term married women, however, won't be shocked. They know my husband is pretty much an average guy. I have yet to meet anyone, man or woman for that matter, who doesn't have their own particular brand of quirk. Given Eddie's many charms, I know I can live with and even feel fond of Eddie's quirkiness. I simply come armed with gloves, a sponge and disinfectant.

The most important things are the values that we share. Finally, at forty-eight years old, after many years of trying to find the perfect guy that fulfils the Hollywood movie and fairy tale promises, I have realized that he simply doesn't exist. I've screened hundreds of men through dating sites, sporting events, social outings, and all places that had the potential to be a PCDS (Prince Charming Department Store). What I didn't realize was that I was deeply immersed in the **Cinderella Fantasy**.

Even Cinderella knows that a regular guy doesn't like doing the dishes and leaves a few dirty socks on the floor now and again, but he is also a leader in his field, who loves his career and who stands by his values even in the face of adversity. Prince Charming can read her mind so all her needs are met without her having to ask. He brings flowers regularly, knows exactly the right thing to say at every moment, rescues kittens out of a tree, helps little old ladies across the street and leaps tall buildings in a single bound.

Sadly, Superman wasn't available but this real human being, a loving man named Eddie, was. It took counsellor training to realize that we are a deeply and beautifully flawed race. For every trait that is attractive in someone, there is usually a dark side. Someone who is a great leader may also insist on always getting their own way; someone who likes harmony may not be able to stand up for themselves; and someone who is proudly self-sufficient may be too embarrassed to ask for help in a crisis, never mind recognize they are in one. The tough part is that so much of our behaviour is unconscious. We act automatically without stopping to consider that another way of behaving might work better. Usually we are willing to try something new only when we find ourselves deeply unhappy.

For a situation to work, it has to work for both people, and no one has to suck it up and stare at a collection of football lighters displayed on the mantle. It's okay and healthy to ask for the cooperation you need to live in surroundings that work for both you and your partner. I am uncovering my own unconscious patterns so I can make other choices and create a new outcome. I tend to be a big dreamer and love to live in Fantasyland. Formerly when my inner fantasy didn't match up with outer reality, **Lizard Brain** would kick in and I would run without explanation. Now I am aware enough to know that when I have the impulse to flee it is a flag to stop and consider something different.

Thankfully Eddie would rather have a meaningful life with me than one with his sports mug, so for him it was a no brainer. Can you imagine if I had let Lizard Brain have his way and run away without giving Eddie an opportunity to accommodate my needs?

As women we often focus on relationships more than men. Being born caretakers, we lean toward being the givers and the mind readers, assessing the needs of those around us, and filling those needs to the best of our ability. We need these skills to be mothers and we expect men to be pro-grammed just like us. "If I just keep giving, he'll give me what I need." When men obstinately refuse to read our minds, we get heartbroken and resentful and the guy, who only a few months earlier looked like Prince Charming, now takes on the loathsome form of a cold-hearted Ogre. It's time for the **Cinderella Fantasy** to go. It's a pattern that keeps women from finding and keeping a successful relationship or from rediscovering happiness with the one we already have.

Kissing our Princes and turning them into toads is so common that women gather together to compare notes on how the fantasy bubble has burst. **Cinderella**, no longer the glowing, precious princess, is back in her grubby clothes scrubbing floors only now there are squalling babies in the background. As in the movie *Shrek*, we need to be careful, as our man might not be the only one with an Ogre lurking beneath the surface.

"He used to bring me flowers and take me to the theatre. Now when he shaves he leaves hair all over the sink and expects me to clean up after him."

"My guy snores, watches hockey all the time and never notices me anymore. Things just aren't the way they used to be."

In any relationship there can be plenty of Ogre-dom evidence to point your finger at. Blaming your guy for turning you into a victim is a mindset that keeps you from discovering your part in the intricate relationship dance.

In an episode of the old TV show *MASH*, Klinger says to Colonel Potter, "I've found myself a woman and now I've got nothing but trouble." Colonel Potter, who has a long-standing, happy marriage says, "When you fall in love, you've always got nothing but trouble. So then you stop loving them or you just decide to love them more."

My trouble and my joy definitely come wrapped up in the form of a lime green plastic covered couch. Let's have a look at how other women opened up to love even with all the trouble.

CHAPTER 2

Cinderella Finds Herself Knee-Deep In The Ashes

Rose's eyes well up with tears as she talks about her relationship with her ex. "I'm still very much in love with my husband. I really didn't want my marriage to break up," she says as her hands clench and her body becomes stiff. "I'm so mad at myself. I don't know what I was thinking." Her fists pound her knees. "I still pine for Ryan." Rose takes a deep breath, "It feels like it was only a short time ago that we've split up, but it's been five years."

Tears roll down her cheeks, she finds it hard to speak, but goes on, "One day, five years ago, my teenage kids sat me down at our kitchen table. My daughter was very angry and upset. My son is more of the stoic kind. He likes to call a spade a spade and this time he was certainly calling one. The family had just found out that my husband had been cheating for quite some time and with several different women, including a friend of mine. This was the last straw for my kids. Their father was mostly absent from their lives and now it was clear why. They didn't like the way he treated me or how he ignored them the rare moments he was at home. They wanted a better life and they thought the three of us could forge our way without him. I understood their point, yet I didn't fully agree with them. I wasn't ready to ask him to leave. I did it out of obligation to them. Now that the kids are grown and gone, if he wasn't remarried I would try to talk him into taking me back. I've lost my chance at a happy marriage."

Rose's face suddenly takes on a dreamy, childlike quality with a hint of a smile gracing her lips. "In my mind I often replay the good times we had together before we were married. My heart would pound with anticipation as I dressed for our dates. I'd try on several outfits to find the one that I thought would take Ryan's breath away. After what seemed like forever, I'd hear the doorbell and rush to find him dressed in stylish Italian clothes, his musky cologne enveloping me as he bent down to kiss my cheek and nuzzle my neck. He would present me with a gorgeous bouquet of my favourite peonies and whisk me up in his arms carrying me off to a moonlit patio for an exquisite dinner. I loved it the most when I got a mysterious note under my door: "Pack a suitcase with a little black dress, heels, some lingerie and not much more. Be ready at 5:00 on Friday and don't expect to be home until Sunday night." The next thing I knew we were flying off to some romantic weekend in Vegas, New Orleans or LA. I didn't stop giggling for months. I felt like Cinderella. My dream had come true. The day I found out I was pregnant was the happiest day of my life. I so wanted to have a family and I was very much in love with him."

Rose's smile suddenly faded away, "I thought Ryan would be as happy as I was, but when I told him about the pregnancy, the blood drained from his face."

"Aren't you happy about this?"

"Of course I am, honey," he said. "It's just a little unexpected."

"He didn't look at all happy, but I told myself he'd soon be as thrilled as I was once he got over the initial shock. I wanted to do nothing but get married and have his children. We were both raised Catholic, so to do anything else would have been unthinkable."

"I was so wrapped up with my babies that I hardly noticed how much things had changed. Ryan became more and more distant. Our fun times stopped and I saw less and less of him all the time."

Tears came to the surface again. "If we could just go back to the way it was before we were married, I know we'd have the best life ever. I want to give it a try."

Two things catch **Counselling Mind's** attention: one is the fact that her children wanted her to leave. Kids will usually do anything to keep their parents together, yet Rose's children could no longer watch their father treat their mother so badly and were tired of being ignored by him. The second thing **Counselling Mind** noticed is that five years later Rose is still grieving the break-up as though it had just happened yesterday.

Rose is caught up in a classic **Cinderella Fantasy**. The cardboard cut-out romantic prince and the real flesh and blood man she was married to are two completely different people. She is pining for a man who is obviously highly skilled at being a suitor and who knows how to steal a lady's heart and how to be romantic as long as he has no obligations. Once "caught," Ryan is a fish out of water and has no idea how to be a good husband or father.

Like Rose, I was once smitten with a fantasy guy, who cut off our relationship abruptly. Yet, he was a pivotal piece in the puzzle of my understanding how we can so easily be swept away by the **Cinderella Fantasy.**

Rod and I had been dating for just a very short time, but there had been lots of fun and plenty of laughter. Then out of the blue Rod called to say he didn't want to go out with me anymore. We were both upset. I didn't understand why he was doing this and there was no real completion or explanation that made sense. He refused to talk to me again or even answer my emails. Like Rose, I was so caught up in the amazing time we had that I missed an important clue that kept me stuck in pain, pining for my prince.

After a few months of not being able to shake the sorrow, I went to see a counsellor.

"So how well do you know this man? Have you met his family or any of his friends?

I managed to snivel out a "No" between tears.

All I knew were the usual details that people share when first dating, the things we like to reveal about ourselves and none of the stuff that we want to hide.

Then she said, "And you also know that he is the kind of guy that will completely cut you off and run away."

That hit me like a ton of bricks. Hearing the truth from someone else brought me back to reality. Yes, Rod was great when we were together; we had a ton of fun, a lot in common and a lot of attraction. He was also the kind of guy who runs away and completely cuts people off with no communication. Both things were real about him, not just the fun side.

The **Cinderella Fantasy** puts a lot of pressure on a man when we continually compare him to the romantic vision we have concocted in our minds. I must have given Rod some notion of what he was going to have to live up to and he bolted before he had the chance to fail.

Just A Little Spit And Polish

Another kind of fantasy that women commonly fall prey to is the belief that a man will become the perfect guy with just a little spit and polish.

Leila has been seeing Rob for almost a year. "He calls me when he feels insecure, lonely, sad or when he needs some comforting. He wants to get close when he feels vulnerable and I rush to his side to be there for him."

Lizard Brain: He had better not be asking for money as well as her time. Leila hasn't mentioned it, but *Lizard Brain* stays alert, ready to throw his arms in the air, just in case.

"When he is feeling good and doesn't need anything, I don't hear from him. He spends his time with his friends and never invites me along. I used to think he would eventually come around and want to spend more time with me, but that's not happening. The problem is I feel desperate for him to love me so I sit around waiting for him to feel needy again. I thought we were falling in love, but someone reaching out to you when they're feeling insecure isn't love. It's insecurity."

Counselling Mind: Good catch, Leila!

Leila hopes that Rob will suddenly become the guy she's always dreamed of.

Leila's role in the fantasy is that of Florence Nightingale, ready and willing, bandages in hand, mending broken hearts everywhere. She's the altruistic caring heroine, loved by all. She's the magnet for the wounded and believes the harder she works and the more often she comes to the rescue, the more Rob will fall in love with her.

Being Florence Nightingale works as long as the patient continues to love and appreciate her. When she no longer is needed, however, Florence becomes the Wicked Witch of the West and all Band-Aids are stripped off with turpentine and eye of newt !

Kissing Frogs

Amanda has similar problems and is unable to see the whole man. She is obviously hoping that her Prince will emerge if she kisses the toad long enough.

"The only time I see Bill is when he shows up and throws rocks at my window after the bar has closed. He doesn't even stay the next morning, but dashes off right after a cup of coffee. He seems uncomfortable being with me unless he has been drinking. He never takes me out on dates or comes to see me any other time. He says he's in love with me, but I want to have more."

Lizard Brain: Throw the rock back at him next time!

Counselling Mind: Lizard Brain! Be nice.

Amanda knows what it's like to have sex with Bill, as that is all their relationship consists of, but she is completely in the dark about any other aspects of him or his life. In actual fact, Amanda is in love with a fantasy with all of her hopes pinned on something that's unlikely to happen. If Bill can only show affection or spend time with her when he is drinking, then she needs to come to the realization that he is incapable of having a healthy, fulfilling relationship unless he gets some serious help.

Jane, too, was caught up in the **Cinderella Fantasy**. "I'm in a relationship with a man who is everything I've ever wanted. I was instantly smitten with Paul and it just seems we were meant to be together. I love his eyes and the way he looks at me as though he was looking into my soul. I love how well we get along and the romantic things he does. We have so much fun together as long as we are alone, which is most of the time."

Counselling Mind: Huh? Why do you only have fun in private? What changes when you are in public?

Jane searches her memory to discern the difference between being home with him and being out in public. "There are other women," she says as a light bulb goes on. "When we are out, he always seems to be talking or flirting with other women."

Counselling Mind: Okay, now we're getting somewhere. Let's see if Jane is imagining this scenario due to insecurity, or if his behaviour is really off base.

"I don't know if I could stand up in a court of law and say, well he did this and he did that. But it feels he is telling women with his body language that he is attracted to them. He is always laughing with them, a little touch here, a wink there, a smile when he thinks I'm not looking. Come to think of it, he always beelines it straight to the prettiest girl in the room, never someone's mother or another man. The next thing I know their giggles are flying across the room. Looking back, I see that it was the same when we met at a party. He headed straight to me and I was instantly smitten with his directness. I assumed Paul was having one of those "There she is, the girl of my dreams' moments." Our dynamic was very flirty. We laughed and talked about everything under the sun for about an hour. I was sensing he was about to ask for my phone number when his girlfriend came to get him and he had to leave.

Lizard Brain: Girlfriend? He was flirting with you for an hour while he was at the party with his girlfriend???

Jane justifies, "But our connection seemed very special. If I met my soul mate while I was dating someone else, I would do the same thing. The next day there was a message on Facebook. He came looking for me. Before long we were messaging back and forth, several times a day. Then he asked me to go for lunch. I asked about his girlfriend and he said it was just a casual, let's-be-friends kind of lunch. Nothing serious."

"I knew in my heart that we were meant to be together, and sure enough it was just like at the party: we laughed and talked about everything. It felt so right. We went for lunch once more that week and a few days later he said he had broken up with his girlfriend. Paul and I could now go on a real date."

"I was so excited. I went out and bought a new dress. He took me out for dinner and then we went for drinks at a comedy club. I'll never forget it. We talked and laughed all night. I knew then that this was the real thing. I had found my soul mate and we were meant to be together."

Lizard Brain: Not likely! You'll probably be the next girl that he dumps once he finds someone who will go out with him even though they know you are his girlfriend.

Counselling Mind: When we start to fall in love, we get completely overwhelmed with feelings. Life looks rosy. It's all hearts and flowers and we are blinded to anything that doesn't fit the fantasy. The pain begins when the etch-a-sketch picture your brain has so artfully drawn no longer matches the real man in front of you.

Jane is holding on to the belief that she is Paul's Cinderella. Anything that does not match that fantasy does not compute for her as this is her blind spot. She believes she is The One for him. The reality was – as it is in most cases like this – that he behaves the same way with all women and wasn't likely to start changing at any time soon. Pain for Jane.

Fantasy thinking is the idea that he is going to be different "someday." The pain begins when you want something more or different from what the relationship is currently offering. When you realize that you have been an equal participant in creating the relationship dynamic, it gives you the power to end the pain. You can direct it to a healthier place, or choose to say goodbye.

Whether you see yourself in any of the scenarios or not, it doesn't mean you're not stuck in a **Cinderella Fantasy**. It's easier to see that the guy is the problem. It's easier to point the finger. What is more difficult is to see your own patterns that keep you stuck and suffering in a loveless place. The indicator is whether you are unhappy and in emotional pain.

The good news is that if you have created the problem, the power to change it is in your hands. It's not saying men don't act badly sometimes, and they aren't responsible for their part in the dynamic. They are. Your power comes when you can start to see your own blind spots. Then you can see how you have attracted the same dysfunction again and again.

Men are neither frogs nor princes. They are human beings with their own brand of baggage. Your task is to learn to dance with the warts that don't go away and start to see him the way he really is.

If your solution to the dilemma is to dump your latest paramour and throw on your headphones to listen to the list-making advice of the current New Age gurus then you and I need to have a serious chat, girlfriend.

(HAPTER 3

The Dreaded List

On the TV show *Millionaire Matchmaker*, Cindy, the featured millionairess, glows with excitement as she walks into Patty the matchmaker's office. She proudly displays the beautiful List she has painstakingly made, as if to say, "I know how proud of me you're going to be as this will make your job soooo much easier."

Cindy, a gorgeous, successful businesswoman has amassed a sizeable fortune. She has just turned forty and is realizing she is now ready for the next conquest: true love.

Her List is a ridiculously large piece of paper, the kind you would buy in an art store. It is coloured in felt pen with artful little pictures and drawings. Given the length of the List, it has obviously taken her some serious thought and quite some time to put together. Cindy hasn't yet found anyone who could measure up to the List (surprising, I know), so now she was calling in the big guns to help. She is sure she is in good hands.

Patty, the matchmaker, recoils in horror. In agonizing slow motion she reaches into her desk, pulls out a lighter, sets the LIST on fire and throws it into the trashcan. Cindy's lip curls up to show her teeth and her eyes glare red – from angel to devil in two seconds flat.

Cindy barely stops herself from doing a head dive into the trash can to pull out her sacred, smoking text which is being burned before her very eyes by someone whom she trusted to help fulfil it. Not a pretty moment in television history.

Imagine Cindy on a first date. In front of her is the list that she holds up so one half of her vision sees the list, the other eyes the potential date, like a split screen. She ticks down the list, yes, no, yes, yes, no, yes, no. "Oh, that's three no's. You're out. Sorry. NEXT!"

Patty understands the fantasy mindset that creates LISTS. She knows she needs to shock Cindy. She understands that people who think like this have a very controlled and specific idea of what love looks like and how it should go. They either reject men on first sight or they find someone who seems to have potential and try to hammer them into the perfect mould they see in their mind's eye. The more defined the criteria, the less happiness and success these women will find in relationships.

Patty burned Cindy's List knowing there is no one on the planet that is able to match up to her fantasy. This List does not give a man any room to breathe or to be the wonderfully flawed human being he is. No one is able to match Cindy's impossibly high standards.

Patty arranges a dinner date at a high end restaurant with a few great men that she has hand picked. Cindy arrives dressed to kill in a skin-hugging dress and high heels, long brown wavy hair flowing down her back and a huge smile on her face. She is on a mission and she is excited.

After she has made her entrance, she says hello to the men and sits down. Her face changes. Fully in charge, she sternly begins the interview, ensuring that everything is going to go her way.

Counselling Mind chuckles and wonders whether Cindi's going to take out that damned checklist. Whichever guy gets the first three strikes will suddenly disappear through a trap-door in the floor.

Cindy begins her interview. The men look stunned. "Wasn't this supposed to be fun? Why do I feel as though I'm at boot camp?" She writes off all of the men within minutes and storms away from the dinner table to confront Patty. "I'm not interested in dating any of these men."

Patty pulls no punches. Patty is a matchmaker who has screened hundreds of men in her profession. She knows a quality guy when she meets one and she has carefully chosen some wonderful men for Cindy.

None of the men Patty picked looked like Hollywood movie stars. They were average looking, normal, good-hearted, solid men. Hollywood movie men all know how to dance, they like shopping, they bring flowers every time they see you, take you to Paris in the spring and pick you up in their Porsche convertible. You are the one true love of their life and they never ever look at other women.

Huh? Have you ever seen Brad Pitt when he isn't working on a movie and hasn't had an airbrush or a shave and a haircut? Movie men are the picture of a woman's perfect fantasy. Hollywood works hard to conjure up escapist moments for us to enjoy. We don't believe that Toy Story is real, but we fall hook, line and sinker for the romance in Titanic.

"You get your butt back to the table," orders Patty. "And open your mind. The idea is to have some fun. Just be curious and see how you feel when you're with them, not if they meet any of your stupid criteria!"

Cindy complies, opens up a little and by the end of the evening she finds one man who, given a decent chance, makes Cindy open up and laugh.

Counselling Mind: It was nice to watch Cindy relax a little and enjoy her time on a date rather than trying to control everything. I'm pretty sure she's going to have to burn a few more Lists and cry a few more tears before she changes her way of thinking.

In the movie, *The Ugly Truth*, Katherine Heigl plays a lovable and more than slightly neurotic control freak television producer who is so desperately single she may as well have a List safely pinned to the front and back of her sweater.

Scene one: Katherine sits at a table in a nice restaurant for dinner with her blind date. He seems like a great guy – smart, funny, open and confident. She immediately tells him that, according to his Internet profile, he fits nine out of ten requirements on her List. She proudly pulls out a copy of her list as well as the background check she has done on him. Before he can open his mouth, she produces another list of topics they can talk about if there are any awkward silences and confidently hands him a copy. His face falls. The message is clear: "This date has already gone on too long and we haven't even ordered dinner yet.

Scene two: Katherine drives home alone and it's still early enough that it's not even dark outside.

Counselling Mind: Even if you're not as brazen as Katherine who hands a List of required traits to her date, men sense when you have a list. They hate being interviewed and scrutinized to see if they measure up. I don't blame them. One thing Katherine had on her Top Ten List is that the perfect guy must like to drink red wine. Think about that for a second. If you finally found someone who treats you like gold, who shares the same goals and values and whose company you enjoy, does it really matter if he prefers a Guinness?

But now, grab your popcorn. We're heading back to our movie.

Katherine's TV station hires Gerard Butler, the hot new television talent. His show is about how men are very simple, sexual animals. His opinion is that if a woman wants a date she should hit the treadmill and wear something that enhances her breasts. Katherine hates him. At the same time as Gerard is hired, Prince Charming moves in next door to Katherine. He's tall, very handsome, chiselled, charming, well-spoken, humble, and down to earth. And he's a doctor! Katherine does the happy dance.

Eager to get it right, Katherine follows Gerard's TV show List about what men want and struggles to turn herself into a picture perfect princess. She pretends to love it when her new date hand-feeds her caviar, but spits it out the second his back is turned. The perfect woman needs to have long hair, so she gets hair extensions. She even wears a pair of vibrator panties to help spice up her somewhat prudish sexual attitude.

As things heat up, she and the Prince plan to take the big step into sex on their next date, but fate intervenes and Katherine and Gerard find themselves in a steamy, passionate lip lock.

Oops! What went wrong? It turns out that Prince Charming is really rather boring. He spends so much time trying to match the List that he really has no character of his own. And Katherine is so busy trying to hammer herself into the perfect woman that the time spent with her Prince is no fun at all. They are both so constrained that there is no spark or passion left.

Gerard, on the other hand, has fallen in love with Katherine, control freak neurotic and all. She's the last person to fit his list. And he's the last person to fit hers.

When Katherine asks, "You're in love with me? Why?"

Gerard responds, bewildered. "I have no idea."

Whenever I ask my husband, Eddie, why he loves me, he says the same thing as Gerard. Isn't it wonderful that love never seems to follow a List?

Many books have been written about how to catch and keep a man. "Girls, if you want to snag your guy, mud wrestle with your good-looking friends, do your man's bidding, cook gourmet meals, stock the fridge with his favourite beer to deliver to him as he's watching the game, and always tell him he's the greatest and that he never does anything wrong."

With the exception of the mud wrestling, I have tried to turn myself into a pretzel, again and again, trying to match what I thought men wanted. I thought I was a failure as a woman and that I was never going to get it right. I finally realized I was just never going to fit that mould.

What these men really want is a Barbie doll, a two-dimensional perfect woman with no needs. This is no different from when we are caught up in the Cinderella fantasy, waiting for our Prince Charming.

Waiting For The One

Greek mythology says the first people had four arms, four legs and two heads. They were split in half to create men and women. Ever after you were always seeking your other half, your soul mate. Only then would you be complete. This is a concept that helps perpetuate fantasy thinking.

More than fifty percent of first marriages end in divorce. If the concept of soul mates is true, don't you think they would find a way to stay together? Wouldn't miracles show up to save the day during challenging moments? Wouldn't there be some mystical power that held you together no matter what?

I know women who think he's The One, when he doesn't even return phone calls. How can he be The One when he isn't thinking she's The One? The whole idea of soul mates is that there is an instant recognition, and that you fall madly, passionately in love with each other and never part.

I've had guys come back to me and say I was their One. "What? You've got to be kidding me! You dropped me like an anchor at sunset the second the hot blonde at the water cooler gave you googly eyes. And now you're thinking I was your One?" Confusing!

I've also been on the other side where I was instantly smitten. The dynamic had been fun, flirty, alive, crazy electric and we really seemed a perfect match. He agreed that we did have this fun connection, but he still wanted to date other women.

Huh? I had been searching for this kind of spark for years! I was sure that when I found it that we would both recognize how rare it was. I was wrong.

We've probably all had more than one One. When I got married for a year at nineteen, I was sure he was The One. I met my next One in my mid-thirties, and eagerly phoned my Mom declaring, "I've found The One!"

"What? Again?" I could almost hear her say.

Many people are onto their second or even third marriages. I bet they would swear on a stack of bibles that they had made a mistake in believing that the last One was The One; however, for sure, their new sweetheart is now really The One.

It's not that the concept isn't sweet. The danger is that you will get caught in another fantasy rather than having a healthy curiosity about who your beloved really is. If you have a set idea about how your ONE should look and act, any deviation from that picture creates upset, confusion and frustration. How could they be The One if they're acting this way? So, you drop them like a hot potato and head off in search of the real One.

In the soul mate scenario there isn't much room for any human flaws, quirks or foibles. No leaving dirty dishes in the sink, no socks on the floor, no wanting to watch the game with his buddies on Saturday night, and definitely no room for a couch covered in lime green plastic. One's don't do those very human things.

Science has finally admitted that love isn't an exact science. Criteria won't make the sparks fly. Instead, love thrives when there is a willingness to give and receive, and it can sneak up in unexpected packages.

With Eddie, I was his One, yet, I can't say the same for him. I didn't spend years pining for him when we split up and I even said, "No," to a date when he called me a decade later. The feelings I have for him are very different from those I had for my Ones. I am very attracted to Eddie, yet I feel less desperate than I used to. I know what I can count on and I know I don't need to change to be loved and cherished by him. My love for him feels more like a warm, contented laze in front of the fire, very comfy and cozy rather than the addicted excitement of never knowing for sure what's going to happen next.

I used to think that "Happily Ever After" meant that a relationship always stayed in that highly charged initial stage of love. Once that first flush of love faded, I assumed my partner was bored with me. As I got more acquainted with the deeper and more stable feelings that love offers, I was finally able to recognize a man who was open, loving and available. I continue to be surprised that Eddie just wants to hang out with me. That's his sweet and simple way of saying, "I love you."

Some women find their man early on in life and are still madly in love with them until the day they die. They could make a good case for the reality of a soul mate.

Is the concept of a soul mate true? I have no idea but what I do know is that learning to embrace the human idiosyncrasies of both partners is a more likely to lead to a happier, healthier relationship than drawing up List after List to see if he measures up, or spending hours analysing whether or not he is The One.

If our parents and grandparents stayed together for their entire lives, it shapes the way we see the potential of The One. Whether they stayed together happily is a whole different issue. Our family culture and messages from our community influence us more than we could ever expect.

(HAPTER 4

Ugly Stepsisters On Your Doorstep

Even if you do find the ideal Prince Charming and your life is going along perfectly, just as in your fantasy, don't be fooled. Your family patterns are ingrained in your psyche and will show up eventually. Out of the corner of your eye, one day you'll see the Ugly Stepsisters, suitcases in hand, coming up your walkway. They know where you live, so there is no escape!

At my high school it was normal for girls to steal each other's boyfriends without a second thought. The strangest part was that it wasn't a big deal. You didn't turf your girlfriend; you just relinquished your guy if he wanted to switch teams.

"Sure, you can borrow my sweater. Oh, my boyfriend? Yeah, go ahead."

It was slightly more covert than that, but you get the picture.

It was not something I would imagine my Mom approving of, yet, after my Dad died while I was in my teens she began a twenty-year-long affair with a married man. My Mom did it, my friends were doing it and I didn't think twice. I did what was acceptable in my family and my culture without question. It wasn't until years later when a friend talked to me about someone who was ostracized for breaking the girl-friend rule that I asked, "Girlfriend rule?"

"Yeah, you never steal your girlfriends' boyfriends."

I was stunned. Loyalty to anyone, including my best girl-friends had not been in my community culture. Although it made sense when my friend said it, and it was obviously the right way to do things for her, it was one hundred and eighty degrees different from what I grew up with.

The Love-O-Meter

The level of emotional maturity with which you relate to relationships is the one you learned in your family and your culture. In other words, you only love as much as you learned how to love. Imagine that you have your own per-sonal love meter, like a thermometer that goes from zero to one hundred. We'll call it a love-o-meter. The amount of love you get when you are young will fill up your love-o-meter to a certain level. If your parents level of love is at thirty, your love-o-meter will only fill up to thirty as well as that is all your parents would be able to teach you. If you had a great mentor in your life, or someone that was a loving influence, it can fill up your love-o-meter an extra notch or two, but everyone in your family and surrounding community is at essentially at the same love level.

You will naturally be attracted to a man who has the same level of love in his love-o-meter. In other words, your capac-ity to give and receive love, or your level of emotional avail-ability will match. Hence, we play our own role in the relation-ship that is equal in function and dysfunction to that of our partner. The degree to which we can get close to someone will reflect in our behaviour, to the same degree as it will reflect in our partner's behaviour.

"What? Noooo! How can that be true? I would never behave like he does. I would not act like him in a million years!" I can hear the screaming now.

You're not alone, girls. It gets especially confusing when you watch a man running around acting like a five-year-old and you can't remember acting like that ever – even when you were five.

It's not that we aren't immature at times; it's just that we are good at disguising it. We have perfected the art of making our immaturity look much more mature.

What is hard to see is our own part in the dynamic. Either we care-take, fight, shut down or be disapproving (my signature move), or we smother our emotions by smoking, shopping, eating, having affairs, over working, etc. Each of us will have our own cultural brand of how we deal with difficult relationship issues. Our behaviour may look different from our partner's, but it still keeps us distant from love at an equal level.

Take Nancy. She's the perfect caretaker. She thinks she's willing and open and that it is her partner who is the problem. "He's the one who's always rejecting me. I keep telling him how much I want our relationship to work and I'll stay through thick and thin. But he's in and out of our relationship like a yo-yo."

Counselling Mind: "Nancy, this isn't easy to grasp or to understand when you're the one feeling the pain right now, but if you weren't invested in the pattern of 'here and gone', 'here and gone,' he wouldn't interest you. You would feel no attraction and you would be in a relationship with someone who is available."

Nancy defends: "But when I'm with him, it's so amazing. I have never felt like this with anyone. He makes me feel so special."

Counselling Mind: "Yes, all of that may be true, as it often is with people that can't sustain a long-term, healthy relationship. Men that do stay in your life aren't as exciting because life isn't exciting at every moment. With guys that flip in and out of your life, it's easy to give a great impression. If he actually stuck around, you would get to see his own brand of faults and quirks. He's afraid to show you the parts of himself that aren't always switched on or perfect. I would bet there is also a part of you that is scared to let yourself be seen for who you really are, when you're not always exciting or at your best. You are just as caught up in this emotional pattern as he is."

Matching Luggage

Along with the level in our love-o-meters, our family rules about relationships, both spoken and unspoken, help create our emotional patterns. No one goes into a relationship with a clean slate. We put on fresh lipstick and get a new hairstyle, but we unwittingly pull our relationship behaviours along behind us in our rolling tote bag. The colour may look different with each partner, but the size and the shape of our baggage is exactly the same. Whether we like it or not, we've got matching luggage.

Take a step back and you will start to notice the level of emotional distance you keep between you and your relationships. Gail's example may help. She is hooked on a man that consumes her every thought. The catch is, she hasn't seen him for seven years.

"Every time the phone rings, I think, 'Is it him?' I watch romantic movies, and envision us as the main characters, so we always have a happy ending. I daydream constantly about the amazing life we had together. I cry as I play the music we used to dance to in my living room, and remember the smell of his musky cologne as we were snuggled together in my hammock, watching the sunset. After cooking dinner together, we'd have a picnic with a bottle of wine in my backyard."

Gail fights back tears. "I still don't understand why he left. It doesn't make any sense."

Counselling Mind: I wonder why a guy would leave a relationship like that. It sounds so great.

Gail continues, "We had this great relationship for about two years and then he suddenly stopped coming to see me. I never heard from him again." Gail's demeanour morphed and she looked like a little girl staring at the ceiling as though she were watching a movie.

"We met when he started talking to me in the grocery store, just like you see in the movies. We are both foodies, so we talked about our favourite foods and shared some of our secret recipes. We laughed and talked for twenty minutes. It was so much fun. At the end of it, he asked for my number and called me two days later to suggest he come to my place and we could cook dinner together. He brought a bottle of wine and fresh cut lilies. Conversation flew and he had me giggling into the wee hours."

"Before I knew it, every Tuesday and Thursday Brad would come over and we would cook dinner. I would spend my weekends looking for new recipes so we could test them together. He would bring different wines to do wine pairings. It all felt very decadent and special. It was a dream come true. When he brought a movie over, sometimes we would watch it and sometimes we wouldn't, if you know what I mean."

"After about a year, I wanted to have more of a relationship than just Tuesdays and Thursdays. He never stayed the night. I was ready to get more serious and asked Brad to spend the weekend with me. He didn't really say much but left that night and didn't come back for a month. He wouldn't return my phone calls either. I didn't know what happened to him. It was like he dropped off the face of the earth." Gail had a little trouble continuing as she was overcome with grief.

Counselling Mind: Here's a tissue, sweetie. I know this isn't easy for you, but it helps to let the feelings go as you tell the story.

Lizard Brain: Did she ever consider that Brad might be married?

Gail wipes her eyes and carries on, "When he came back, he was more romantic than ever. He said he missed me like crazy but he was building a business and didn't have time to take things to the next level yet. He told me he has to be up early for work so likes to sleep at home and needs to work on weekends. He asked me to be happy with the way things were. I didn't want him to stay away like that again, so I agreed."

"After we had been together for another year, I was invited to my friend's wedding. I was so excited. Brad and I had never been out of my house together before, so this was a chance to do something different. I wanted him to meet my friends and I thought it wouldn't kill him to take a few hours off for once. When I asked him to go, he didn't really say anything. He just mumbled something that didn't make sense. The real answer came when he walked out the door that night and never showed up again. That was seven years ago and I still don't know what happened. He was the perfect guy. I couldn't have asked for anything more."

Counselling Mind: Yes, you could have. You could have asked for a guy that was ready and willing to have a real relationship with you. It's easy to look perfect when you only spend ten hours a week with someone, especially when most of that time is in the bedroom.

Gail revealed more as she continued. "Brad reminded me of my Dad whom I loved so much. He travelled for business, so he wasn't home very much, but when he was home he was lots of fun. He always brought my Mom flowers and a present for me. He would take us to the park or the zoo. He also loved to cook and we would spend time in the kitchen baking cakes and trying out new recipes. It was great. He was pretty much the perfect Dad."

Does this sound familiar? Gail is used to the men in her life being gone most of the time and only there for the good times. For her, men can do no wrong, as she never gets to see their bad side. They always pop in and out of her life with a smile and a bouquet. The sad part is there is never any depth. Gail never gets to see a man be a real human being and she's used to feeling a lot of love for a man who is rarely around.

Not all intimacy patterns are as obvious as Gail's or as glaring as women who were beaten as children and are then attracted to men who beat them. Wouldn't it be perfect if everyone walked around wearing T-shirts that declared: "I'm commitment phobic," "I'm clingy," or, "I've got an anger issue." There is no way to know for sure the specifics of a relationship dynamic until you get to know your partner better.

People with parents who didn't show them love or affection, were distant or who constantly criticised them, often find partners who do the same. Or they themselves become critical because they need to replicate the emotional distance they grew up with. In my first marriage, my husband would regularly tell me women were stupid and inferior. Criticism was a normal thing in my family, so I tolerated it and also dished it out. I was equally ingrained in the dynamic.

Emotional distance can take on many different disguises and it comes in varying degrees. It could look like a long-distance relationship, an affair with a married man, someone whose work schedule keeps him away or dating someone with a big age difference so you have little in common. These circumstances leave little room for any kind of sustained emotional engagement.

What is key is the level of distance you are familiar with. You will be attracted to someone whose upbringing matches your comfort level without realizing why. You call it love because that's what love looks and feels like to you.

Cathy had been seeing a guy she really liked but he was only available when he had nothing else scheduled, rather than making her a priority. When she asked him to step up the level of importance of their relationship, he said, "No."

She continued to date him, realizing the dynamic had a strange familiarity to it.

Cathy describes waking up to her relationship patterns: "It was as though my brain had been in a fog. All my life I had been satisfied with tidbits of love from men. I realized that this pattern had started with my Dad. He was the cool, silent type and I was used to only getting tidbits of attention. That was all I was able to give back to others. It felt normal to me."

Through counselling, she discovered she was afraid that if someone was around too much, they would see her unlikeable traits. Once they saw who she really was, they would leave. By choosing men who weren't often available, she felt she was protecting herself. But in reality all she was protecting herself from was having a fulfilling, long-term relationship.

The Ogre And The Princess

Shannon fluctuates between anger and tears. "How could I have been so stupid? I have been with my husband for twenty years and I can't believe he cheated on me! In fact, it turns out he has probably been cheating for our whole marriage. How could I have not seen the signs? Why was I so blind?"

After talking to friends Shannon discovers that, although empathetic, most of them weren't surprised. Shannon continues, "My best friend Susan said, 'He always had an eye for the ladies, and even though I had no proof, it just doesn't come as a big shock.'"

"Other friends have said similar things. It's so confusing. How could they see it and I couldn't?"

After being discovered, John came clean about his infidelities. He loves Shannon and asks if she is willing to get help rather than lose the wife he loves. After some soul searching, Shannon agrees.

Counselling Mind: An important first step is to explore what they both want and will work for their marriage and what won't. But it's not the only step. If this is all they do, they will miss a big opportunity for both of them.

It's easy to look at John as the bad guy and that is generally what the world does. Poor innocent Shannon – her man has cheated. There's John, suddenly the Ogre.

It's not that John's behaviour wasn't out of line. Yet, this is the perfect opportunity for Shannon to see her own relationship patterns. She held onto her "everything's perfect" fantasy with such fervour that it didn't allow her to see the signs that John was cheating. If she is attracted to someone who is a serial cheater, it is likely that this is a pattern that runs in her family and was imbedded in her psyche long before she met John. And this is also a pattern that likely ran through John's family and was imbedded in his psyche long before he met Shannon. He fitted her pattern and she his – hence their attraction to each other. To unravel this will take some deep, rich exploration, struggle, and time. She will start to see the level of distance she is comfortable with, learn to fill in her blind spots, develop her own inner sense of security and fill up her love-o-meter. The good news is they both love each other and are headed in the right direction.

When you finally get frustrated with the old patterns and decide you want a healthy and effective relationship, it will take some time and self-discovery. If you don't take the leap then you are doomed to stay in the teenage love phase of dreaming of a perfect man that will always elude you. Release that mirage back into Fantasyland, find yourself a real man and start to create a healthy and real relation-ship. This requires that you accept your part in creating both healthy and dysfunctional relationships.

Pollyanna And Hitler

In one of my darker moments of trying to find the perfect guy, I stumbled upon Bob. He imagined things that hadn't happened or he would embellish a situation so that it no longer resembled reality. Looking back, I realized he had some kind of psychosis. He was always the one going off the deep end and it was easy to see that he was the one who had the biggest issues, wasn't it? I couldn't see how we matched and denied the idea that we had to be matching in our love/distance levels.

While struggling through this issue and complaining bitterly about Bob, my counsellor tossed me a small bomb: "So what made you give him your phone number?"

Clunk. Penny drops with a thud, light bulb goes on, bells and whistles sound, and smoke comes streaming out my ears. I had known Bob in a social setting and I was the one who suggested we date. Looking back I had to wonder what had attracted me to him. Was I really so uncomfortable about being close that I chose someone who was psychotic? Was my love-o-meter really at such a low level? It was hard to fathom.

I think back to some of his crazy behaviour and to a friend's warning: "I've never met anyone who seems so uncomfortable in his own skin." The only thing that makes sense is that I was blinded by the dreaded *Cinderella Fantasy* and I was terrified of getting close to someone.

I think of myself as a loving, open and willing person who sees the good side in everyone. Little did I know at the time that my Pollyanna nature would put me into a scary situation where I had to phone the police to stop Bob from pounding on my front door and yelling threats through the mail slot.

Even Hitler had a long-term partner, Eva Braun. From the world's perspective, Eva could write a book about what a bad guy he was and all the terrible things he did and many would agree.

Counselling Mind: Yes, that's true. And it's not as though Hitler was a handsome, sexy guy with women falling at his feet. I can't imagine what love must have felt like to her if she was attracted to him. And what would make you continue to stay in a relationship with a maniacal killer?

Damsel In Distress

It's all too easy for women in relationships to see themselves as the "wronged" ones. Let's take a quick look at some of the common wrongs women blame their men for:

- "He cheated on me." Take a good long look at your family history and you will likely find a string of men (and women) who cheat when things get tense. You will find yourself attracted to a cheating type of man or you may find yourself running into another man's arms when you are feeling bored or unloved.

- "He's mean." Again, look to family patterns. Were you yelled at, criticized, or ignored? You will recreate this pattern in your own relationship, even if you are the one who is being mean. If a man isn't being critical enough, you will unconsciously find a way to make it happen and blind yourself to your role in the relationship drama.

Until you learn how to increase your own love-o-meter level, you will keep repeating these unhealthy patterns using escape behaviours to create dysfunctional relationships similar to the ones you grew up with. Are you the one who needs to fight back? Are you always the understanding one? Do you shut up, shut down and silently resent your partner? Drinking, adultery, binge eating, working too hard, or relying too much on your kids or others to meet your emotional needs – all of these are escape behaviours that keep you stuck at the level of distance you grew up with. Although the behaviours may vary, what does match is your love-o-meter, or your comfort level with the degree of emotional closeness and distance.

What I found most confusing about the theory of matching emotional levels was seeing immature and reactionary behaviours in my partners. I was certain I would never behave in such childish ways. Eventually I noticed that I was reacting to their reaction by getting mad, judging them and pointing out inappropriate or embarrassing behaviour, or having some kind of hissy fit.

For example, your boyfriend flirts with another woman at a party. On the way home you find a way to point out how inappropriate his behaviour was. You yell, or you talk in a stony, measured tone, or you cry. Your guilt delivery method may vary but what's really going on is that your reaction has equalled his behaviour. That is the indicator that you are matched in your love-o-meter. What you are doing is pushing him away by making him the bad guy.

When you choose not to get hooked into the situation, and don't have an emotional reaction, the relationship starts to change. You begin to make better decisions about what you can do for yourself. You talk about how his behaviour makes you feel and what's okay with you, or not, rather than making him the bad guy. The best part is the level in your love-o-meter goes up. You get to feel good about you and you get to see if he is open to making some changes and respecting your boundaries. Then, depending on his response, you get to see if the relationship really works for you-or not.

Being the nurturers of society, women often care-take or rescue others. This makes us look like the wonderful heroine and casts our partner into the role of being the immature boy–man. The problem is that the more we do this, the more we reinforce our emotional distance level. (These roles can be reversed; the issue is the same) Al-anon is a great place to learn about enabling behaviours and the signals we unconsciously give that tell our partners when their behaviour affects us in a way we don't like. Clearmind calls it over-functioning and it takes on many clever guises.

Cinderella, Put Those Cleaning Gloves Down!

Stacy wins the award for caretaker of the year. She did everything for her husband, Luke, down to ironing his underwear and re-arranging his dresser drawers so they were always neat and tidy. All he had to do was come home, watch TV and zone out. Did it make a difference to Luke that his underwear was ironed? No. None. He couldn't have cared less.

But it was Stacy's way of over-functioning in order to keep an emotional distance. She was too busy to connect with Luke on any real level. When things got too close, she'd get out the vacuum. Yet she got huffed when he didn't do the extras for her like bring her flowers or surprise her with dinner at a nice restaurant. "He doesn't do anything. I do it all." That may be true, but it's because she has set it up that way. Her over-functioning gives her the perfect ammunition for being right.

The catch of over-functioning is that she is so busy looking after his feelings, his needs and correcting his behaviour that she never addresses her own. She expects Luke to be able to read her mind and proactively look after her desires just as she does for him. This wishful thinking keeps her (un)comfortably at the level of emotional distance she is used to.

Stacy comes from a long line of female over-functioners armed with household cleaning tools and a yellow plastic gloved wrist dramatically placed on their foreheads. She learned how to do relationships from her mother and her mother's mother, just as she learned how to keep her home spotless.

An overriding cultural message in North American society that keeps us distant from each other is the idea that something outside ourselves is going to make us happy: money, success, fame, a nice car or the perfect relationship. I call it the fantasy of The Thing that will make life finally work.

CHAPTER 5

Gotta Be Me, So You Gotta Go

Hugh and Gail Prather propose some interesting theories about how the rapid changes in society are affecting our relationships in their book, *I Will Never Leave You*. When the rebellion of the sixties kicked into high gear, the values of society changed. Things moved from the cultural value of keep-your-family-together-at-all-costs to the Me generation. "I need to find myself," "I need to feel empowered," and "I need someone that will listen to me."

In post-war North America, consumerism had become the buzz of the day with the introduction of television, mass marketing and mass media. Now, you too, can own a jar of make-everything-look-shiny-and-perfect.

Picture the American dream: the smell of the roast beef simmering in the oven wafts through the air as Mother mixes peas and grated carrots into green jello for a lovely aspic. Mmmmm.

"Kids, Daddy's home!"

Billy and Sally come running down the stairs, excitedly. "Daddy, Daddy!"

"Now, no running, kids. I've told you this before. And remember to say thank you for the hula hoop and yo-yo Daddy bought you."

"OK, Mommy."

Dad hangs up his hat, gives Mom (fresh dress, lipstick and hairspray) a peck on the cheek and then bends down to give the kids a hug.

"Hey Slugger, how's that baseball swing?"

"Swell, Dad."

"And, how's my little princess?"

"I missed you, Daddy."

Sheesh. Somebody please wake me up. I was going to go on about everyone snuggling in front of the TV, tummies full after a slice of Sara Lee cake, to watch the Wonderful World of Disney, but I'm starting to feel a little queasy.

In order to emulate the Beaver Cleaver façade of a perfect, loving family there are a lot of hidden rules that go hand-in-hand with this way of life. Any deviation from the *proper* behaviour cannot be tolerated, often indicated by subtle corrections such as a raised eyebrow or an ahem clearing of the throat. After a while these behaviours become programmed in our brains. In time, we don't even need our parents anymore, as our own minds take over, silently repeating rules we don't even realize we are following: "Say please and thank you," "Your hair is a mess," "You can't go out wearing that," and "What will the neighbours think?"

We become our own worst critics and our minds pounce whenever we dare stray one iota from the hidden rules. These become blind spots and because they are invisible to us we unconsciously look for an unsuspecting culprit to blame – usually those who are closest to us: "YOU are the one making me unhappy."

Depending on our sibling position and the role we take in our family, we either become the keeper of the rules or the one who doesn't want to follow them. The catch is, the only way to break free from the clutches of all of these pervasive family rules is to break them.

Cue the sixties.

No wonder the hippie generation happened. The Beaver Cleaver fifties would have us pretend to be nothing but squeaky clean happy all the time. To keep up this façade, it's necessary to clamp down on every feeling we have that is not happy. As human beings we naturally feel a range of emotions so eventually the repression has to erupt like a long dormant volcano. And it did. The Me generation exploded with a fury of passion and experimentation.

"After two failed marriages and one failed eight-year relationship I've discovered that I'm just not the marrying kind," claims a famous Hollywood starlet. "I blame my father for not showing me what a good man is."

Our upbringing plays a major role in our psychological makeup and why we are attracted to certain people and not others. Understanding that is step one. Yet, if you really want a fulfilling relationship, it's necessary to take stock of what you're thinking or doing that is keeping you stuck. We often think that something outside ourselves is the reason we're not able to choose a good partner or have a good relationship.

The buck doesn't stop here. It's a pretty powerless position when you have no choice but to continue making the same mistakes over and over, never learning from them and then blaming your parents. Our parents and our grandparents' generation didn't think this way. They didn't jump from relationship to relationship, saying, "You're not the one. Oh, not you either. Oh, you especially suck, I'm outta here." Divorce was rare and even scandalous in their day.

Born in 1962, I was pretty good at Me, but by the time I was forty years old and had been through dozens of he's-the-one-oops-no-he's-not relationships, I realized that doing Me all the time wasn't helping me find what I yearned for. I knew I needed to learn a new way of doing things, but I had no idea where to begin. I just knew I had to find some middle ground between the attitude of the Me generation and the-family-at-all-costs, a perspective I was surrounded with growing up with and finally realized I had been rebelling against all my life.

Author Hugh Prather tells the story of Andy and Rachel, whose marriage was a casualty of Me generation thinking – always looking for what "I want" without considering a larger perspective. Decades earlier they would have been envied. They had the ultimate life and a breakup would have been unthinkable. People who have fifty-year marriages go through some tough struggles, both together and personally. Yet they share a common value: they are determined to make their marriage work, no matter what. They are staying. Period.

Although Andy and Rachel loved each other, still had regular, good quality sex, kids they adored, careers they enjoyed and more than enough money flowing in, they were both discontent. They weren't "finding themselves" within the confines of the marriage. Their solution was to blame the institution and eventually dissolve a great marriage.

Counselling Mind: I'm confused. It breaks my heart that they were unable to identify that their restless feelings were their signature way of keeping a comfortable distance from each other. They missed the opportunity to grow with each other and take their love-o-meters up a notch.

What's Your Thing?

Andy and Rachel thought The Thing that was going to fulfil them was being single, as their marriage was not The Thing they expected.

Sometimes The Thing can present itself in unexpected ways. At the Diva-do, a local charity that supports the Big Brothers Foundation, the most coveted item they had at their silent auction was a jersey from our local hockey hero, Ryan Kessler. Ryan is the kind of manly man who makes women swoon as if they were Scarlett O'Hara in a southern heat wave.

The hormonal frenzy in the air was palpable as women put in bid after bid for the coveted icon. You could practically see the thought bubbles above each woman's head as she pictured this perfect, sensitive athlete skating up to her after scoring the winning goal in the hockey game and planting a big heroic kiss on her eager lips, then sweeping her into his strong, protective arms to carry her off into the sunset.

Sigh.

Before you can say Zamboni, a room full of women were madly typing into their iPhones, arranging second mortgages so they could be the one to develop a deep, meaningful relationship with this piece of fabric.

Caught up in the frenzy, the jersey looks like The Thing that is going to make someone very happy. And then comes the moment they announce your name and you become the lucky princess of the hour. You step up to the podium to become the keeper of the iconic jersey, all eyes jealously on you. All is right with the world. You are the winner of the fantasy frenzy! All women want to be standing in your stilettos! Life rocks and your love-o-meter is filled up to one hundred!

The next few days are great as you can feel the joy in your full love-o-meter as you phone all your friends and family and include them in the fantasy frenzy.

"You'll never guess what happened!"

"OMG, I'm coming right over!"

For the first month, you wear the jersey to bed every night. After a month, you hang the jersey on your bedroom wall where you get to say goodnight to it every evening and good morning as soon as you wake up. Your love-o-meter is down to eighty, but still feeling pretty good. After a few weeks, you barely notice the jersey. Down to sixty. A few months later, the jersey is getting a bit dirty and dusty, so you pull it down, wash it, and put it away in a drawer. Every few months you take it out and remember your glory moment, but the memory has faded. After a quick shot of jersey adrenaline, your love-o-meter returns to default mode.

Whether we are shopping, eating, going on holidays, starting a new friendship or adopting a pet, each time we think, "This is it!" But, after the initial flush of excitement and when it comes time to maintain The Thing, or it is replaced by the next Thing, it's no longer glamorous, nor is it keeping the love-o-meter at one hundred.

We treat our relationships as though the next one is going to be The Thing that answers all our needs in one fell swoop. In reality, a relationship needs care and nurturing through all the ups and downs that life throws our way.

Author Debbie Ford describes this beautifully: "Maybe you believe that life should be better than it is this day. You may believe that you should be more, better and different from the way you are, and you probably expect others to be more, better and different from the way they are. This mindset causes you to be dissatisfied. It causes you to get on the proverbial treadmill and chase one more thing in the outer world that promises to give you inner satisfaction. But it is a cosmic joke, a twisted paradox – because if you really do find something to fill the hole for a while, you will be seduced into believing that you can fill the hole from the outside in. Then you are sucked in, for what seems like an eternity, to trying to find the next quick fix to satisfy the hole in your soul. On the other hand, if you do not find the thing to fill the hole, you are tricked into believing that you will be satisfied the moment you do find that one thing that will fill it for a while. So in a sense, you are screwed either way. You are damned if you do, and doomed if you do not, to living a life of wanting and waiting for the great fulfilment to come your way."

Initially it feels really good for the person who has become your next Thing. It's great to be seen in this romantic glow of near perfection. But what happens when the **Cinderella Fantasy** no longer fits?

For me the bubble-burst moment usually happens around the six-month mark. The man who was going to be The Thing suddenly is not. One hundred to freezing, in one second flat. How could he be so human? After the bubble burst, my signature move was to torture him for a further year and a half reminding him constantly about how disappointing he was. I would stay for two years gathering enough incriminating

Ogre-like evidence to justify my inevitable departure. It's no wonder both of us eventually shut down.

Linda learned a tough lesson about The Thing. "When I was young I had an amazing, torrid love affair with a very romantic man. We did all the things that women dream about – picnics in the park, dinners by candlelight, and walks along the beach. We had been dating for about four months when he ended the relationship abruptly. He said his decision was non-negotiable and he wouldn't change his mind. I was shocked. I asked him what made him come to this decision."

He said, "Linda, I could swim across the ocean, walk across the desert and climb the highest mountain to get to the top, pick you a dozen red roses, then do it all in reverse order to get them back to you. At that point you would notice that there were yellow roses at the top of the mountain, so I would do it all again but this time bring you back the yellow roses. That wouldn't be quite right because now you would want white roses. After all was said and done, you would complain because you really wanted the pink roses."

"I was stunned, but in my heart I knew he was right. I was happy with what he had done for only a short time and then I'd get my mind set on some other Thing he needed to do so I could feel happy. That breakup taught me a valuable lesson. I thought it was up to him to fulfil my needs exactly as I wanted rather than being grateful for what he did."

In Linda's fantasy, all she could see were the roses she didn't get rather than appreciating the beautiful ones she had received. She missed out on what he had actually done for her. Her constant demand for something more was her way of keeping the comfortable emotional distance of her default love-o-meter. She was unconsciously pushing away the love she really wanted. Sounds like a tough lesson learned.

During the honeymoon period, all you want to do is be with your new love. Friends and family fall by the wayside. You used to go to girlie movies every Wednesday, now you stay home so you can hang out with your new Thing. As your love-o-meter fills with your latest obsession, it's easy to mistake it as a permanent state. It is, however, no different from when your love-o-meter is temporarily filled by the fantasy of the Ryan Kessler jersey, or when a good marriage ends because you think being single is the answer. Eventually your love-o-meter will reset back to your habitual comfort level.

Until our love-o-meter is full, the empty part will always make us restless. Yearning for love, we reach out for a piece of chocolate, a new pair of shoes, accolades for our latest achievement, or the next relationship. If you regularly have conversations with yourself about how you will be so much happier when you are thinner, when you have more control of your life, when your bank account is overflowing, or when you are in a relationship, or when you are out of the one you're in, see if you can notice it and do something else. Give yourself a break from this ongoing mind craze and go have a hot bath instead. Believe me, you'll thank me.

While you're soaking, consider this: Every time you think something or someone is The Thing that is going to make you happy, make a mental note. What you are really pursuing is happiness. The good news is there is a way to find it.

When John Lennon was young his Mom told him, "Whatever you do in life, always make sure you are happy."

One day, John's teacher asked his class what they wanted to be when they grew up.

John said, "Happy."

The teacher responded, "Son, you don't understand the exercise."

John replied, "You don't understand life."

Money, a perfect body and a perfect relationship are the top three must-haves that women believe will be their Thing. It took me three years in a counselling program to discover what you've probably already figured out – relationships are my Thing! I went into the course thinking I needed to get better at being in a relationship. What actually came to light was that I realized it was my way of thinking, not what I was doing, that was keeping me from happiness.

The happiest people I've met are the ones who have a spiritual path. They think differently, and have different values and place greater importance on nurturing vital, supportive and loving relationships than those who are driven to pursue The Thing. They have unlocked their secret to increasing the temperature in their love-o-meter. Their fulfilment is in what they do, the things they look for in their lives to be grateful for, and their rewards are in simple things. They are the first to reach out with loving kindness. They are not bothered about what others think, as they are know who they are in their hearts and they like what they find there.

I recommend that you start to get curious and learn to identify the particular way in which you push love away to a comfortable distance. By understanding that the ball of change lies in your court, you can start to live from a place of inner rather than outer happiness.

CHAPTER 6

Blinded By The Sparkle Of The Glass Slipper

"But I have this gift of seeing the best in him and seeing his greatest potential." The penny dropped! I had heard this before. In fact, I had said this very thing myself many times along with:

"Oh, one day he'll be all he can be."

Or:

"If I just keep telling him how great he is, one day he'll get it."

That last is my favourite. We think our ability to see our partner's higher possibility is very spiritual and mature. While it is lovely to see the best in people, it also can be the hook that keeps us in the fantasy of The Future Promise. The last time I heard, "But I have this gift..." was when an acquaintance told me that her husband was leaving her for another woman after twelve years of marriage. She was blinded by his potential and not fully understanding the man was heading out of the door with his suitcase in tow.

The trouble comes when there's a disconnect between wanting to see the best in your partner and the behaviour they are demonstrating right now. It's as though a veil of deception fogs over our eyes and we are unable to see what's really going on.

Sheila showed me a photo of the man she was dating. I recognized him as a former acquaintance that I had known as a fun-loving, intense guy. Yet the photo showed that something wasn't quite right. When I knew him he had been well kept and nice looking but his picture showed a very overweight man wearing clothes that looked worse than his long straggly hair.

Sheila sighed. "He promised he would cut his hair, lose the extra weight and get back to his old self. He's a lawyer and he's trying to get a job in his field again, but hasn't been successful so far. He says he loves me and wants to take me to Bali when he gets back on his feet. The confusing part is we've been seeing each other for six months and nothing has changed."

Lizard Brain: Danger! I'm getting nervous! It might take time to lose weight, but he could have had a haircut and new clothes yesterday!

Sheila continues, "I've seen old pictures of him. He looked great and I know he's been successful in the past. I know he has it in him. Once he gets on his feet, he'll be great."

Then rather reluctantly she adds, "He said he is planning to quit drinking and doing drugs soon."

Counselling Mind: Aha! That would explain why he looks the way he does and the reason he hasn't kept any promises.

"Our life will be so great when he gets a job. We're going to travel and have lots of fun. He'll look like Brad Pitt. We'll win the lottery. He will quit drugs and alcohol overnight. He will start a shelter for addicted children in third world countries. And we'll live happily ever after."

Okay, she didn't say this last bit, but this is essentially the disconnect from reality that typifies the Future Promise.

A Future Promise looks lovely. Unfortunately it's a **Cinderella Fantasy** that will never be realized. You imagine you can turn your guy and your life into exactly what you want. The sad truth is that years are spent living with nothing more than the bubble of hope. Nothing changes. In fact, the more time goes by, the more pain and heartbreak you suffer. The more time goes by, the more pain and heartbreak you suffer. And, no, that's not a typo.

It can be difficult when Mr. Future Promise keeps telling you what he will do but somehow never gets around to. Of course, women also make up their own Future Promises, even if a guy hasn't promised anything.

Does The Prince Charming Suit Fit?

Deborah was really attracted to Chuck but Chuck told her up front: "I don't have much time to spend with you, as my kids are still young and in my life a lot. I'm only available Tuesday and Friday nights."

Lizard Brain: Let me translate what he is saying. "Hey you're cute! I don't have much time to put into a relationship, I just want something casual, and this is all I'm willing to give right now. You in?"

Counselling Mind: It was great that Chuck was so straightforward. He is being up front about what he wants, and is looking for someone who wants the same thing. Good for him. It's not that this might change if Chuck falls in love while he is dating casually, but it's not something you can count on or count on at any time soon. If you are looking for a serious relationship right now, Chuck is not a good bet.

Deborah refuses to hear this. Although she is looking for a long-term relationship, she likes Chuck, and damn it, she's going to turn herself into a pretzel and be a patient martyr while he spends the next ten years with his kids.

Checking in with Deborah a few months later, the truth is now hitting home. "I'm really struggling. I'm in a great deal of pain as I'm quite smitten with Chuck but he isn't able to spend any more time with me than what he originally promised. I find myself lonely and pining for him when I know he is spending time with his kids instead of me. I told him I'd be happy to go with all of them to the park, but he isn't ready to introduce his kids to anyone he is dating. I'm starting to resent the kids. Chuck feels pressured, so things are difficult between us."

As you can see, Deborah is still hooked into the Future Promise. She is hoping he will change his mind as time goes by. He hasn't. He is committed to what he had originally said.

My husband, Eddie, thinks Deborah should watch the movie; *He's Just Not That Into You.* He says, "If a guy is really interested, he'll move mountains to find a way to make a relationship happen. If he's not, move on. If a guy starts out saying he's not very available, why would you run full speed into his arms?"

The Future Promise is a blind spot that many of us have. If you have a pattern of dating unavailable men, take note because this particular brand of the **Cinderella Fantasy** may be one of your unconscious relationship patterns.

Counselling Mind: If a guy is serious, he will say with both words and actions: "I'm ready for a long-term relationship. I like you and would like to spend time with you and only you."

Lizard Brain: Yes, I agree. If you don't get a straight answer when you ask about his intentions, there is a good reason for that. My advice: Move on and find someone who is available.

With counselling Deborah took a step towards getting more clarity for herself. She told Chuck she was interested in spending more time with him. He stuck to what he originally said. This told her that he's just not that into her or that his time really isn't flexible right now. Either way he's unavailable for the kind of relationship Deborah yearns for. The mistake is hanging in there, hoping the cosmos will rearrange itself, the angels will sing and the stars will align so that the Prince and Princess can live happily ever after.

It's not easy to walk away, but if Deborah truly wants a long-term relationship then she needs to cut her losses and deal with short-term pain rather than being unhappy and dissatisfied for a long time.

Instead of taking the time to date and be curious about who the other person really is, the Future Promise says jump first, ask questions later, or actually, never ask the questions at all. Even if your highly charged hormones are telling you otherwise, until you get to know a man's life, his friends, family, and workplace, you are still in the very early dating exploration stage.

Lori could have used a reality check before she got too involved with Wes.

"We met on the Internet and sparks flew immediately. Our first date was lunch – a meet and greet to see if we liked each other. We did. Our second date was at a gorgeous restaurant on the waterfront, then for a drive to the beach afterward. We sat in his car, talked and kissed until the sun came up. It was the best date I've ever had. We both agreed we wanted to keep seeing each other. But then he didn't call for two weeks! It seemed like forever and he was a bit evasive when I said I would have liked to see him sooner. I then decided I'd better talk about what we were looking for in a relationship to make sure we were both on the same page."

Counselling Mind: Good idea to do a reality check, Lori.

"I told him I was looking for something serious. He told me he was just out of a long-term relationship and wasn't ready for another one yet. He wanted to find the person he would spend the rest of his life with, but meanwhile he wanted to remain single and see who is out in the playing field."

The tough part for Lori was that she was already hooked. All she heard was that he was "going to find the person he was going to spend the rest of his life with." She did catch that he intended to date other women, but the idea that he was looking for that special one became her obsession.

"I decided I was going to get proactive. I'm going to make me the chosen one. It's going to be me that he falls in love with."

This was where all hell broke loose and the pain began. After only three dates she was already determined to make the Future Promise a reality.

Lizard Brain: You don't know a man after three dates! He could be a psycho killer!

"I had tons of fun and spent hours thinking up cute little emails to send, but then waited for days until I finally got a short and sweet response. I planned elaborate dinners yet when I invited him over, he wasn't available. Fretting that he was out on other dates became horribly painful. When he did call, I'd hit the malls and buy a new, sexy outfit, get my hair and nails done and spend a great deal of money I couldn't really afford. If he said he liked the colour red, I would buy a red dress. I bleached my hair because he said he liked blondes. I was working hard to make him want me."

Lizard Brain: That reminds me of Stacy, the underwear ironer who was always going overboard while expecting her guy would reciprocate. At least Stacy was already in a relationship. Looks as though Lori is working hard for a maybe, kinda, sorta Future Promise of one.

"Suddenly I felt like something snapped and I woke up from a bad dream. I was sitting by the phone on a Saturday night, which I would never do before I met him. I had given up most of my activities so I could be available in case he called. The anticipation was electric. I felt alive and excited if there were a chance he would call, yet as soon as I realized he wasn't going to, I would plummet down into pain. I had been spending every minute in either complete hope or complete despair. I had never felt so much pain over a guy and had never tried to be someone I wasn't before. No matter what I did, it didn't make any difference. He still wasn't making any further commitment to me."

"One thing I noticed was that he never went out of his way for me. In fact, the more I wanted him, the more he backed away. I was happy when he would throw me a tidbit of his time and I was in pain when we weren't together."

Luckily for Lori, the penny dropped when she realized she was the one making all the effort and was getting little back. This was her first step to standing up for herself and moving on.

Stop Kissing That Toad!

Emily didn't get off quite so easily.

"My instincts were screaming at me, but I overrode them because I wanted the Future Promise of marriage and a family so badly," said Emily, still shell-shocked.

"My relationship with Mark was amazing for the first year. I met him at an event at my country club and we hit it off immediately. We went out for dinner to a nice restaurant every weekend and on excursions to spas at least every other month. After dating for a year, we took a trip to Hawaii and then decided to move in together with the idea that we would be married the following year. I was ready to settle down and start a family and Mark seemed like my dream come true. He always paid for everything we did, so I assumed he was financially secure. He said he had a good job as a consultant and was always flying around the country to meet high-end clients, or at least that's what he told me. Now I don't know for sure."

"After we moved in, Mark wanted to put all of our finances into joint accounts. We still had a year before we were to be married but for some reason my instinct said, "No." When I told him, he got very upset. He was starting to show a very different side. And I didn't like it."

"I was hoping to just let it slide for a while, but he was relentless. He kept saying, "If we're going to be married, we have to share everything and we have to be able to trust each other.""

"I trusted him until he started going on and on about how I don't trust him. Trust is a very important thing in a marriage, and I never thought I would be with someone that wasn't trustworthy. My guts kept screaming, "No!" but I only saw the dream and did what he wanted.

The anger in Emily's eyes was apparent. "The next thing I knew, he completely cleaned me out and was gone before

I could blink. I lost a large chunk of my money. Now I know how he could afford all of those extravagant dinners and weekends. He likely did that to some other woman before me."

Her anger was turning to tears. "I don't know how I could have been so stupid. I was really in love and blinded. The police haven't been able to find him. My clock is ticking and I'm not sure if I'll ever be able to open my heart to anyone again. I'm starting to give up hope."

No one wants to be in Emily's shoes and most would say she is the victim to Mark's deviousness and dishonesty. The catch is, if we continue to think like this, it keeps us stuck.

Dr. Phil McGraw states plainly, "There are no victims, just participants."

It's clear that Mark was up to no good. So where did Emily go wrong? How could she have suspected this would happen? She could have listened to her instincts when his behaviour changed and he started pushing her to share bank accounts. What do you think Donald Trump would do if a woman started pushing him to share his bank accounts? Could you imagine Donald being worn down to give in to a pushy woman and not sign a pre-nup? It's just not in his character, like it is in Emily's. Donald's financial advisors would probably quit before they allowed it.

Even though Emily was in love it is never a good idea to make decisions based on the *Cinderella Fantasy*. The support of a lawyer, a financial advisor, a counsellor, or friends and family members she trusts would likely have saved her a lot of pain. Without knowing the facts she essentially let herself be manipulated out of her money.

Promises, Promises

My husband Eddie has a passion for finding free stuff and then selling it on Craigslist. We have an agreement that whatever he brings home to sell has to fit into the storage locker or his walk-in closet. I have to keep on top of it or else my whole home will be filled with things Eddie plans to sell someday. He would leave a skinny path through the apartment, but otherwise we would be living in a "Bunny-look-what-I-found-to-sell" jungle. When I notice that the storage locker and Eddie's closet are full and the free stuff he's sure will sell like a hot potato threatens to take over the second bedroom, I ask him to please clean it up. He promises and promises, but soon I'm greeting the bric-a-brac like house-guests that have overstayed their welcome.

One last, "Bunny, I'm going to run over and pick up some stuff right now – they're giving it away for free!" is the straw that finally breaks the camel's back.

"Where are you going to put it? Your closet and the storage are already full."

"I promise I'll clean out my closet soon so I can fit it in."

Eddie can be awfully charming when he wants his way, so I usually cave in and just say, "Yes." I mean, who wants to look like the bitch from hell? I put up with it until eventually, while picking my way through a pile of junk in what used to be my spare bedroom, I turned into the Wicked Witch of the West.

This time I saw a way to break out of this pattern. I perched on the leg of an upside down coffee table that he was sure would sell "in a snap" beside Eddie and said, "I know you have good intentions, but you have been promising to clean out your closet for months. You are making me promises for the future while asking me to make another concession today. I don't believe you're going to keep your promise. You know I go crazy and get cranky when the house gets too cluttered and, guess what sweetheart, you're the one who has to live with me."

His closet was cleaned out that afternoon. And he got to bring home even more free stuff. We were both happy.

One of the biggest lessons I learned about the Future Promise is that people sometimes play by different rules. I had a man tell me, "I feel so alive when I'm with you. We just seem so connected. Our dynamic is incredible. I can't believe how gorgeous you are!" To me, those words suggest something permanent. Something you would say to someone if you were falling in love.

My roommate chatted with my date before we went out and said to me, "That's going well. He really likes you."

"Yes," I said, "but he still wants to date other women."

She looked at me stunned. "I can see why you find this confusing. That's not the impression he gave."

This is why I love getting feedback from others. Up until then I knew I was confused, but was so caught up in the **Cinderella Fantasy** I didn't want to face that he was giving mixed messages. My roommate's comment made me wake up and realize this was probably a pattern for him. The only way to know for sure was to ask him.

His response was, "Well, that's how I feel about you in the moment."

It made me realize he was probably saying these "in the moment" things to all the women he was dating and that he and I have very different rules when it comes to considering other people's feelings. I knew our values were just too far apart in our perspectives. I stopped trying to turn myself into a pretzel to make him fall in love with me and took **Lizard Brain's** advice: Run!

Sympathy Can Be Bad For Your Health

Barb had been dating Paul for a few months, but lately his behaviour had become violent. He would explode in a rage at the slightest thing, and even though he hadn't hit her (yet), he would go nose to nose with her and threaten to.

"Oh, but I understand why he's like this. His Dad beat him as a child and he never got the love he needed. When he's not angry, he's really very sweet and loving."

Lizard Brain: Sheesh! What's the deal with all this understanding? Do women think leaving yourself vulnerable to bullying is a mature or spiritual way to be?

Many women empathise easily, putting themselves into another's shoes. The problems start when they put themselves fully into someone else's size 9s while leaving their own Mary Jane's empty. In other words, they give someone else complete understanding but don't save any for themselves. In Barb's case this could land her in the hospital, or worse.

Right now Paul is testing Barb's boundaries to see how far he can push them. Because Barb isn't saying, "Stop," Paul is reading this as a green light. When Barb does not stop him and lets the situation escalate, she's being a willing participant.

One thing I can guarantee is if you see behaviour once, it's likely to be repeated. Being understanding without a firm "No" will get you more of the same every time. If you think about it, you will start to see how you create your own monsters.

For example, your man does something you don't like. We'll call it behaviour A. You understand. You stay with him and don't say or do anything about it. Behaviour A happens again, but now behaviour B is added. You like this even less, but you understand why he did it. Still you stay and don't say or do anything. Then comes behaviour A, B plus C. This scares you and you cry. He apologizes. You feel better and you understand. You kiss and make up. Still you stay and don't say it's not okay. Now, behaviour A, B, C and he punches you – behaviour D. You're in the hospital.

If you are the kind of person who would not have tolerated behaviour A in the first place, your chances of ending up in the hospital are greatly diminished. If he is invested in the relationship and understands you would stop seeing him if behaviour A happens again, he would make his choices accordingly. If behaviour A is a normal habit for him, it would be a good idea for him to get some counselling and even better for you to not get too invested until you see changes in the right direction.

(Please note-I am not trying to diminish your experience in any way if you have been on the receiving end of violent behaviour. You deserve to have a true, loving relationship and I want you to know that it is available to you. My goal is to outline the one of many potential patterns pattern so you can see how it's possible to have a new experience.)

In the movie *The Rainmaker*, Matt Damon's character is a young lawyer who tries his first case against a corrupt insurance company with a huge team of equally corrupt lawyers. He wins and then decides to quit law. He explains, "I looked at the lawyers for the insurance company and I realized that this business can easily make you become someone you dislike. One day you cross a little line, and then the next week you cross another little line, and then the next week you cross another little line, and then suddenly you become someone you don't even recognize and the line doesn't even exist for you anymore. You look back and you wonder, 'How did I get here?'"

A solid partnership with respectful boundaries on both sides can keep both people on track, especially when they don't realize they have crossed a line.

After reading about others who got stuck in the Future Promise or thought that the next relationship is going to be The Thing or spent way too many Saturday nights revising their List, you are probably wondering, "Now what? What can I do about it?"

Be willing to face your fears and let go of the crutch of the Hollywood fantasy. Put your life jacket on, get ready to jump in the water and doggie paddle your way into the world of grown-up love.

Understanding your own family dynamic is a step in the right direction to find out what's going on because unconscious patterns play a big part in how we relate to others. It's a good idea to install radar that detects the **Cinderella Fantasy** before rather than after you get whisked off your feet.

CHAPTER 7

Free Milk And A Cow

Like any government, business, or institution, a family runs on rules. They can help life go more smoothly or be confining if their impact is not seriously considered. Some rules are obvious, some are inferred.

Here are some of my family's more memorable rules:

"Men won't buy the cow when they're getting the milk for free." My mother's voice rings out as if it were yesterday. As a woman, your mandate (pardon the pun) is to get married. That will give you the security you need, and security is really the goal. It's your only goal. Don't get too involved in anything else in life because you have to drop it all when you get married.

A man's job is to bring home the bacon, mow the lawn, put out the garbage and take the car in when it needs fixing. A woman's job is to be serious and take care of absolutely everything else. Men get to go out and enjoy themselves, so make sure they take you for some fun once in a while. Just make sure you have some way to exert control over men, or anyone for that matter. Guilt works well.

Kids are a burden, not meant to be enjoyed. They especially should not behave like kids. A kid that behaves like a kid is a brat. Just sit quietly at all times and "Do what you're told. Do what you're told. Do what you're told." The ideal child wants to do nothing but housework all the time. Imagine a seven-year-old yelling, "Hey, who's hogging the vacuum?" A mom's dream come true.

Naturally, I've amplified these subtle, hidden messages for effect. My family didn't walk around saying these things aloud, and when they read this it will confirm that I am as crazy as they always believed I was. In truth, I had to dig to discover these family rules. The more I dug, the more I learned about why I related to love the way I did. It was an important step in helping me change the patterns that were keeping me away from love. My family history may help you understand that what is not being said overtly in your own family may contain hidden messages that continue to control you.

Bowen's Family Systems Theory is a tool counsellors use to highlight unconscious beliefs that can run through a family's culture for generations. Our lives and our behaviours are controlled by these invisible patterns.

You can come from an open or a closed family system. In an open system, the family works to support the success and individual expression of each family member. Members are encouraged to learn by taking risks and making mistakes. This gives them flexibility in dealing creatively with any number of issues that life throws at them. The system works because everyone's individuality is acknowledged and they, in turn, want to support the well-being of the entire family.

In a closed system the individual's needs are not considered first. It is each member's responsibility to do what the family wants and support the family in the way it has traditionally been done. It is a much more restricted structure with lots of guilt and lots of rules. In a closed system, everyone follows the rules because taking risks is unsafe and mistakes are punished. "Do what you're told, follow the rules and you will be safe." The only way out of the system, the only way to do something different or choose your own life path, is to break the rules.

In *The Winds of War*, a great, historical novel about World War II, a mother and father are meeting their son, Byron at the train station. Byron has just come from Poland, freshly invaded by the Nazis. He was trapped there during Germany's invasion, had been shot at several times, narrowly escaped death, starved, had to risk his life simply to get water, and had his passport and luggage burned. He was lucky to escape alive.

As he gets off the train, his mother exclaims, "Byron, you look terrible!" The impression is that she is referring more to his appearance than his health. Although she cares about her son, this woman is very concerned with looks and what others will think.

Byron is from a closed family system and the message is clear. The first concern is not about Byron's welfare, but about how Byron looks and how that affects the family image. In fact, Byron doesn't exist as an individual entity. His existence serves one purpose – to be a reflection of the family. As he gets off the train having barely escaped death, it's nonetheless evident that he's not doing a very good job at maintaining a good family image.

Reading the scene I feel my inner rebel rise up and shout out against this skewed sense of priority. Unfortunately, I can imagine my own mother and her mother and her mother's mother saying something exactly like that. If I were in his shoes getting off the train, even though I was at death's door, I would be straightening my hair and checking a mirror to ensure that I didn't look too unsightly. To this day, I automatically obey the voice of the generations of matriarchs before me that is deeply programmed into my mind. It requires insight to see that this is a programmed response, which then allows me to make another choice.

Once you uncover your secret family rules, you start to see what made you the person you are today. You either follow the family rules or you rebel against them. When you know what is driving you, your choices about what you really want become clearer. You also gain empathy for others in your family as you realize that the same rules have been passed down from generation to generation.

When discovering some of my own family rules, it was clear that there were some messages in them that were difficult for me to adopt, yet the value of the exploration was exponential. As I explored my family's losses, I got to see why the rules were made, which made it easier to understand and forgive them rather than fight them. The intent of the rules was initially to protect the family members from future loss, rather than just to control people for the sake of it. As time goes by the rules are still unconsciously followed even if they become outdated, unnecessary or are even a bit misguided.

Bucking Or Buckling Under The Family Beliefs

I am the youngest of four girls. My older sisters were born in the forties and fifties. I was the caboose who showed up in the sixties and may as well have been born on a different planet. At almost nine years younger than my next sibling, I am considered both a youngest and an only child according to Bowen's Family System's Theory. The youngest are rule breakers, freedom seekers and rebels. Only children have a sense of responsibility that would normally fall to an oldest child, hence I became a rebellious caretaker.

My sisters were raised in the post-war era when there were strong family values. To them, I looked completely selfish and irresponsible. My era was peace, love and let it all hang loose. Their lives looked oppressive to me.

Coming from a British lower working class family background, women were expected to finish high school (a newer development), find a husband, buy a house and have babies. Life was simpler; women stayed home to raise the kids and maintain home life. Not only was it what you were supposed to do, it was The Thing. Fulfilment and happiness were not something you should even think about.

Only spinsters had careers. Options were limited – you could be a teacher, a nurse or a secretary. These careers were approved wifely duties out in the world. Coming from the rebellious sixties, it looked like head down martyrdom to me.

There was no higher education, no travel, no passions explored, no personal development of any kind. Tow the line, cook the dinners, do the laundry, procreate. Given these guidelines, I was expected to go out into the world and find a man. So like a good girl I finished high school and got married at the requisite age of nineteen. It probably won't come as a surprise that it lasted less than a year. Whether I knew it or not, I linked up with a man who fitted my family's love-o-meter level to a T.

Looking back at my marriage, I realized I had learned a co-dependent relationship pattern from my family culture. The more love I gave, the more I took care of my guy, slathering him with whatever he wanted, whenever he wanted it, the more I assumed he would become dependent on me. He would see what a great wife I was and would reciprocate. Then miraculously, he would change into the man I really wanted to be married to – someone who could read my mind and give me what I needed to be happy. No surprise, I kept getting heartbroken and disappointed over and over again.

The irony is he thought he was behaving just fine. Since I kept doing what he wanted, there was no reason for him to change. All seemed well in his world. He believed fully that women's work was women's work. And I complied while he sat on the couch with his feet up.

But times they were a-changin' and we now needed both of us to work to make ends meet. The catch was he still expected me to do all the shopping, cooking and cleaning as well as hold down a full-time job. I didn't like this deal very much, but felt compelled to follow the loud voice of my cultural rules, "Women are supposed to do all the housework. It's our job."

Instead of being able to have a mature discussion with my husband and ask him to contribute, the rules would scream that he was right. Naturally the rules of those times were screaming to my husband as well. He would regularly announce that women were stupid and inferior to men. He constantly compared me to other women and I was never as good as they were. What a dreamboat.

I played along, the willing victim to this bad guy, following my family pattern. Not realizing that the rules were blind spots for both of us, I rebelled against the rules and blamed him as the culprit, following the lead of the rising feminist movement. It wasn't until I made up my mind to leave our marriage that I finally told him that it was difficult to stay with a man who said cruel and mean things. Yet, from his perspective, this was normal behaviour in his family. Knowing what I know now, it was obvious that we would be attracted to each other as our specific brands of dysfunction fitted together like puzzle pieces.

Years later I ran into him and he said he had fallen in love with another woman who broke up with him for the same reasons. When he heard the same feedback a second time it gave him incentive to change.

Another decade later, I saw him again walking down the street, holding hands with his pregnant wife. Public displays of affection were not tolerated in my day. I was happy to see he had grown and he hadn't given up on love. Some people would never have risked it again. As bad as some of his behaviour was, he really did love me the best way he knew how. Our family cultures dictated the level of our love-o-meters which were starting to clash with the changing times.

After my marriage I got my degree in serial monogamy and became a master at two-year relationships. I had completely bought into the Hollywood fantasy that happily-ever-after was supposed to last forever. As soon as things got tough or tedious, I was out of the door so fast that I barely had time to jump into my pumpkin. I did this for about twenty years until the heels on my glass slippers were worn down and I knew I needed to trade them in for a pair of sensible shoes. I was tired of going through the heartbreak of failed relationship after failed relationship.

I was in love with the idea of love but I wasn't any good at sustaining it. I didn't know what real love meant for that matter. Giving a man everything he wanted without having any of my own needs met and then blaming him for the situation was my pattern. It certainly wasn't working but I didn't understand what to do differently to feel satisfied.

A big turning point was at age thirty-four when I fell head over heels with a guy I met playing volleyball on the beach on a sunny summer day. He was fun, handsome, tanned and I was smitten. We had the most amazing life I could have imagined. We had a huge group of friends and we were always doing something outrageous and fun. Skiing, kayaking, mountain biking, camping, travelling, going to concerts, music festivals – anything you could think of that was adventurous – we were doing it.

We were great together and people looked at our relationship with envy. This was it! When you meet The One all of your life falls into place and then...happily ever after happens! I thought the rest of my life would now be a hopscotch along the yellow brick road. And just like Dorothy, I wasn't expecting that the wizard would be a fake.

The honeymoon lasted about a year and then we struggled through three more years together. The empty parts of our love-o-meters started to get the usual stirrings and we played out our family rules on each other until we blew the whole thing apart.

When that relationship ended a piece of my heart closed down. It felt like my love-o-meter was down to zero. I shook my fist at God. "God, if this isn't The Thing, then, tell me what is!"

I didn't know who I was or what I wanted, and dated a bunch of men whose love-o-meters were also down to zero. It was a rough time in my life.

At forty, I was ready to settle down to find lifelong love. That was when all hell broke loose. Every man I met was now a potential husband, so the ante was upped, The List in hand, signed, stamped and written in triplicate. This illusive husband became my new Thing.

Unfortunately it all left me feeling empty. After eight years of pain, confusion, struggle, many, many dates, lots of dating-site exploration (I've tried them all) I found a new perspective, and only then did I finally find love. In fairness, it was those eight years of struggle that made me realize that I had to open up and be vulnerable in order to find lasting love. It took the outside perspective of counselling for me to see that I was like a kid trying to learn to read without a teacher to make sense of the squiggles on the page. Without that help I would still be searching or I would have given upon on love altogether.

The deeper my spiritual journey went, the more I wanted to share who I was with my prospective suitors. Instead of trying to please them by telling them what they wanted to hear so they would be impressed with me, I was completely honest. I risked telling the truth. My List was no use anymore. Instead, my gauge was how I felt when I was in their company rather than some insignificant detail.

Some men would turn themselves into a pretzel for me when I honestly shared who I am. I got to see from the other side how unattractive that is and I noticed my knee-jerk reaction was to criticize them. It made me understand why men were critical with me in the past, and how I encouraged it with my own behaviour.

Some would badger me into becoming their picture-perfect woman. This had worked in the past because I learned that criticism was what getting attention looked like in my family. I now began to take a stand and was no longer willing to live like that. I was certainly not going to continue to be open and vulnerable when someone was being nasty. Like the proverbial light bulb going on, I realized that allowing someone to treat me badly was not being understanding or an act of love, it was destructive for both parties. In fact it kills love faster than anything else and is a terrible foundation for a relationship.

Other men would get speechless when I shared myself and would stare at me like a deer in the headlights. One man could tell that I was insightful, but he didn't get "all that kind of stuff." He said he was just a simple guy and he wouldn't be able to match me. I agreed and our first date was our last. He wasn't interested in self-discovery or in learning anything about me for that matter. I found that with a few men. If we spent more than a few dates and he hadn't asked anything about my life, it was a flag that he really wasn't interested in who I was. He preferred the fantasy in his head and didn't want to risk bursting his bubble by getting to know a real person. The *Cinderella Fantasy* is a two-way street.

During this whole process of screening, chatting, meeting, dating, and exposing myself in the process, I would carefully watch my own reactions. I checked in to see whether I felt like opening up and exposing more of myself, or whether I felt like closing down and stepping back. If I felt open I would go out with the guy again but if I felt closed, that was it. I found some men were immediate, instinctive "No's." I stopped questioning myself because my instincts were always right. I found that I was drawn in by some men who said all the right things but when I asked about dating exclusively, the tables would turn. One guy got very controlling, another wanted to be Casanova and date other women, and another ran away as fast as he possibly could. While it felt difficult to let go of a relationship with a smooth talker, I knew it wouldn't get me what I wanted in the end. I chose short-term sadness over long-term dissatisfaction.

On my first date with Eddie the second time around, he immediately told me that he was scared he was going to get hurt again. His vulnerability was refreshing and my reaction to him was indicative of where the relationship could go. The old me would have wanted to see if I could snare him again, to see if I could fill my need to be desired. The new me had to convince Eddie that I was a very different person from the one he knew twenty-two years prior. I was serious this time. Luckily, he was willing to see if I would live up to my promises.

It was easy to love and to allow myself to be loved with Eddie. There were no mixed messages, no big Future Promises, no dances of unavailability. We were both ready, we were both willing and we were both committed. There was never any doubt or confusion.

Eddie fits my family culture in many ways. He is stable and reliable. He tows the line and is a good workhorse, doing his job and earning money the way a man is supposed to. When he comes home, he does the manly stuff but has never learned to do the womanly stuff. The difference is that his family members treat each other with more kindness than mine.

My family culture is to be hard on each other, not interact much or show much love or affection. If I described the way love felt to me in my family, it would be "guarded." Distance was maintained by being critical and learning to accept criticism. It was a mindset that likely helped my family to survive on some level. "Don't get too close, you could get hurt." But it didn't bring any of us closer together or give us the skills to enjoy a life built on loving relationships.

With Eddie I've found a man who fits my culture enough that it feels easy and comfortable. And through my own growth I am now able to accept and meet his loving kindness.

Exploring your family culture and rules will be a big eye-opener. You will discover patterns that have been passed down from generation to generation based on what threatened the survival of the family or its members – deaths, financial misfortunes or dark family secrets. It makes it easy to understand your family's particular brand of rules. In many families women who got pregnant before they were married were ineligible for marriage because not only were they deflowered but now there was a child to be cared for. It could mean destitution, not only for the young woman but for the whole family. The rules were made with good intentions but become problems when they continue to guide the family when times have changed. The milk and the cow became out-dated with the invention of the pill.

A family system, just like a love-o-meter, yearns to be opened and allowed greater freedom. Both good kids and rebels serve a purpose and are unconsciously cultivated, with each member of the family playing a part. The golden child upholds the family values, which will stay intact until the family rebel challenges them. But no matter whether you are fighting them or complying with them, the best way to make new rules is to make peace with the old ones first. This will help change the level in your love-o-meter.

Learning about your family helps find forgiveness for the members in it. You realize your parents, or the sibling you continue to quarrel with, are part of the system and are doing the best they know how, based on the rules. The more you understand that the family rules were set up for protection, the more your empathy will affect everyone's love-o-meter.

Forgiveness for yourself and for others, just the way they are, is the key to peace and contentment.

I saw that my unhappiness was linked to my sense of help-lessness when I couldn't change others and continued to fight my family rules. When I decided I was tired of leaving relationships, of finding a new place to live after every break up and of suffering the heartache of loss, I had a good long talk with myself. I make a hard decision and followed it up by getting out of my comfort zone and doing things differently. Now a whole new world has opened up.

CHAPTER 8

Glass Slippers Ain't That Comfy

*"If a woman is always feeling disappointed
by the man she's with,
either she's with the wrong man or she's not
ready for a relationship."*
~ Anonymous.

I've learned that every human character trait has both a positive and a negative aspect. For example, Eddie is a soft-hearted guy who melts me with just a look. He wants people to like him and doesn't like to fight. The downside of not putting up a fight is that he doesn't take a strong stand about things that are important because he would rather be liked than argue.

I'm a recovering people pleaser and as my love-o-meter got filled, I no longer overrode my instincts and started to speak up in the face of adversity. One day Eddie was being very insistent that I go to the bank with him. The bank had called and he needed to make a decision about a new term for the money in his RRSP. I was busy and didn't want to go, but he was very stubborn about it.

Finally I asked him, "Why do you want me to go so badly?"

He said, "Because if they offer me a free TV to do what they want, I'll take the TV and you won't!"

I couldn't help but smile all the way to the bank. On the other hand, what makes me decisive also makes me think that I know what is right. It doesn't always allow room for other people's opinions.

Women in successful relationships and marriages recognize that every personality trait comes with two sides. Instead of criticizing what they don't like – which is my family pattern – they choose to see what is great about their man and pay more attention to that than what is "wrong" with him. They make small, everyday decisions for love and take care of their own needs in areas their man can't.

A friend of mine says if you want to let go of something old, you have to replace it with something you want more. If you really want a great relationship, you have to be willing to let go of the *Cinderella Fantasy* and install real people in the place of Prince Charming and his perfect Princess cut-out.

When I did this with money, it was substantially easier than discovering my relationship patterns. When I was tired of being broke and struggling, I finally sat down and thought about what was different when I wasn't stressed about money. I thought the answer would be making more money. But it wasn't. The times I felt struggle-free was when I was managing my money well. I got my priorities straight and when I went to make a purchase that was outside my budget, I would ask myself if it was worth the stress. My choice was the gorgeous new sweater in just my size and colour, or no money stress. As tempting as the sweater was, and even though I was caught up in the excitement of buying it, I was so tired of the stress that I chose to keep my money in my wallet.

The same thing happened for me in relationships. I had had enough. With love, however, it looked like unchartered territory with no clear road map. Luckily, I was in year three of my counselling program, so had all the support I needed to make some serious changes. The first thing I needed to do was make the decision for love, once and for all. No more shiny Future Promises or sparkly Things in the shape of unavailable Prince Charmings to distract me from my goal. I stayed committed to finding long-term love by walking away from anything, or anyone, even if it looked tempting, because I knew it wouldn't get me what I wanted.

Oh, But The Ogre Is So Cute!

At the beginning of the new season featuring Ashley as the new *Bachelorette* on the popular TV show, she reflects on last year's heartbreak. "My relationship with Brad, last year's Bachelor, was getting deeper and deeper. I had fallen for him and he kept telling me that his feelings for me were growing, but before I knew it, he said it wasn't working out. I was quite shocked, but looking back, I'm not surprised."

"At the time I couldn't really believe that he could be in love with me. I never once told him how I felt because I was in a competition with two other women. My lack of confidence was my downfall. I didn't really think he would choose me and in the end my insecurities won. I'm grateful I now have a second chance at finding love. I really want this and I'm going to do what it takes to make it happen."

I was riveted to the TV to see if she would find a way to let love in. I was rooting for her. The producers had picked some great, quality guys, any of whom could be a good match for her.

Each of the contenders said essentially the same thing – they were established in their careers; they had dated around and were ready to fall in love and settle down. All except one guy named Bentley. Bentley talked only about himself and didn't mention Ashley or being serious about falling in love.

Ashley is warned by a friend, "I know Bentley. He is coming on the show to promote his business, not because he is interested in you." Ashley responds with, "I just hope he's not really good looking and nice."

Counselling Mind: I don't know what her definition of nice is, but in my book, it's definitely not a person that is deceptive, especially when people's deep feelings are at stake.

By the second show, Ashley says she's falling for guess who – none other than Bentley.

By episode three, Bentley makes a surprise visit to her hotel room. He says, "I miss my daughter and I'm going home."

He isn't honest about the real reason. Behind the scenes he tells the camera, "I feel as though I've already won the competition, but I'm just not that into her."

Lizard Brain: So here you are, Ashley, with twenty-four hot looking guys, all ready to fall in love with you, and you beeline it to the one who isn't interested. I smell danger!

This is an interesting choice point for Ashley. She has chosen the very thing that will be too emotionally expensive for her. She wants the flashy new sweater even though it doesn't fit. She can give up and pine for Bentley, or she can decide she really wants to find love with someone who is able to love her back. This is where she can make a choice for love.

It's likely that Ashley felt she had to compete for love and attention in her past and therefore anything that is hard to obtain feels like love to her. For starters, she put herself onto a TV show where she has to compete with other women for one guy. Now she has chosen the very man who isn't available. All that looks like hard work to me!

Bentley shows up episodes later saying he wants to talk to Ashley again. It appeared that he was testing her to see if she was still hot for him. Luckily Ashley had examined the situation and could see through his game. She asked him some direct questions and he gave confusing, mixed-message answers. She walked out, shutting the door firmly behind her, and didn't look back.

Lizard Brain is jumping up and down, clapping!

Ashley found love with a great guy in the end. After Bentley left the first time, she had a good cry, felt her frustration, punched a few pillows and then she got back on the horse and kept going. She made a decision for love instead of wallowing in heartbreak.

Screening For Keepers

The process of standing for love is the same if you are in a relationship. July Ono, a successful Vancouver real estate investor and educator, has a great love story of her own.

"In honour of our ten-year anniversary, I am reminded of that fatefully charmed, serendipitous day when Steve and I first met. I didn't want to go to a friend's party at the Vancouver Club and Steve was invited at the last minute but almost didn't show up. So there we are, two people who had no plans to be there, and yet the angels conspired to ensure that we met. And when we did, it's been fireworks ever since."

"Let me back up to ten years earlier. There was this other guy in my life that I was head over heels for. He seemed to be serious, but was giving mixed signals. So I wrote a love letter to generate a response. I got a response all right – he dumped me."

"I consoled myself by sobbing over a chocolate milkshake. By the time I finished the shake, I was as right as rain. Little did I know that I would soon meet the love of my life. I wanted to know if Steve was serious, so took out the same love letter and switched the names out. His response was completely opposite. He embraced me with open arms, elated to find someone else with such conviction. "You're exactly the woman I've been looking for."

July is a risk taker. Even though she was head over heels, she was willing to see if her boyfriend was on the same page. She got her heart broken the first time, yet she made a firm decision for love. She was willing to lose what little she had (and it is very little when love is one-sided) to gain what she really wanted. This time it paid off. July and Steve are still together and have a thriving business.

Learning to love a new way isn't always easy. It means being willing to back down from an unsuccessful pattern and take the time and self-reflection to explore new ways of relating to others.

Initially it can be really uncomfortable, and rather than following our habitual anxiety-covering responses, we can learn to express ourselves, our fears, our dreams, our loves, our losses, from a place that invites love rather than pushing it away.

One of my struggles was learning to identify the Long-Term Guy. What kind of things do they say? How do they spend their time? How will I know for sure? Flip the page and let's dissect this rare species.

CHAPTER 9

What The Heck Does Long Term Look Like?

Depending on which stat you read, women over forty-five have anywhere from a .04% chance to a 25% chance of marrying. Whichever one it really is, the number diminishes considerably as we age.

I did almost a decade of Internet dating starting in my thirties and it was not the **Cinderella Fantasy** I imagined it to be.

Why was dating so much more difficult the older I became? In my twenties it seemed there were men everywhere. At any party or social event there was plenty of choice. Then, as I got older, not only were the gatherings less frequent, but there were fewer and fewer single guys.

One day a light bulb went on: "Hey, Marion, did you notice that the reason there aren't any eligible single guys is because the long-term family men are already married?" The now brightly shining light bulb revealed the disturbing truth that if I had been ready for a long-term commitment, I too would be married by now. I was busy pointing the finger at the commitment phobes of the male world and...yikes, I now saw that I needed to lump myself in with them. That was a bitter pill to swallow.

I pictured myself at a CPA (Commitment Phobes Anonymous) meeting. "Hi. My name is Marion. I'm a commitment phobe. If I strung all my two-year relationships back to back, I would have been married for twenty years! But now I'm forty years old and my chances of finding long-term love are becoming slimmer by the minute."

My pattern was to find fault with my mates so I could leave them before they dumped me. Deep down, I didn't believe they wanted me long term and I thought I was doing them a favour by leaving.

Davidji, a meditation master, describes a new way of looking at this dilemma:

> Suppose you are dissatisfied with your job (or your relationship) and want to find a new one. You start looking through the newspapers (or Internet dating sites) and talking to friends who are familiar with your career (plight), but nothing turns up. You might become frustrated and your inner dialogue might conclude: "There's just nothing (or no one) out there for me."

> Observe how this experience contrasts with another example from a very different part of the world. Suppose a hunter in the Amazon rainforest is having difficulty finding game. If he goes to a shaman to deal with the situation, neither the hunter nor the shaman looks anywhere but within the hunter himself for the solution to the problem. It never occurs to them to say something like, "There's no game (or good men) out there," because they know there

is. The problem is that something within the hunter is preventing him from finding the game. Maybe something in the hunter is even driving away the game. So the hunter asks the shaman to participate in a ritual that is designed to change what is in the hunter's heart and mind because it is the heart and mind that control the external reality.

In the glaring light of that irritatingly truthful light bulb, I realized that I didn't have the skills to maintain a long-term relationship. I knew how to dress in eye-catching clothes or flirt if I wanted to turn up the heat and catch me a short-term guy. It struck me that guys in the same boat knew what it took to draw me in, but lacked the skills for a long-term partnership. We were the pretend-we're-having-fun leftovers in the world of marriage.

But What The Heck Does A Long-Term Guy Look Like?

Gary, a friend of mine, was a perfect example of a long-term guy. He had been happily married for twenty years when he was shocked by his wife asking for a divorce. He quickly found another long-term relationship with his girlfriend, Cheryl. She is a travel agent who is often away for up to two weeks. He said he doesn't mind one night alone – he can eat pizza, have a beer and watch the game – but any longer than that and he misses her and starts to get antsy. I didn't even know that men like this existed. I thought every man would jump at a chance to have his girlfriend away for weeks at a time and was shocked when he said he missed her.

I'm not like him. Nor are the guys I tend to be attracted to. What was I going to do? I now had new relationship skills, yet was programmed to be attracted to short-term men. It's not that long-term men aren't out there; I just had to learn how to identify them and find one I was attracted to.

Is He For Real?

Sarah Rowlands, a Vancouver dating columnist, describes the difference between a long-term and short-term guy.

> I hear so many women these days say, "He's a nice guy" as though it were a bad thing. This is usually right before they dump a stand-up guy because he's not exciting enough. As a preacher (and a practitioner) of the "don't settle" philosophy, I find this particular trend quite disconcerting because I believe my mantra is being grossly misinterpreted.
>
> For the record, I'm not saying you should ditch that nice guy who's really into you for a sinfully lustful connection with an exciting bar star who keeps you on an emotional roller coaster because you never know where you quite stand with him. Sure, you'll never have a dull moment if you invite that kind of dynamic into your life. But you'll never have peace of mind or true love, for that matter.
>
> Nice guys never string you along, but non-committal guys will send the following message: "I want the same thing as you,

babe, just not right now. So hang in there because I may get around to meeting your needs at some point down the road." It may take you a while to realize that "some point down the road" is never going to come.

So when you do have your revelation about nice guys, don't think you can hone in on the nice guy you've ditched and swoop him away from the woman he's currently with. Nice guys keep their commitments. That ship has sailed.

This really spells it out: "If you spend too long holding onto the one that treats you like an option, you'll miss finding the one that treats you like a priority."

I discovered that it's important to learn to spot behaviour that isn't above board. When we first start to date, we put our best selves forward, which is normal behaviour. But where is the line between someone putting their best foot forward, and someone misrepresenting themselves? It's a matter of degree. If you are trying to be your best self, you amplify your best traits. Fair enough. Misrepresentation, however, is concealing that they aren't interested in pursuing a relationship.

- A misrepresenter will make their exes out to be crazy, but will fail to mention they were the ones whose unreliable behaviour drove the ex crazy.

- People in the normal range will do things like wear their best clothes and lingerie, and eventually you will see the comfy robe and slippers.

- Misrepresenters will make a point of telling you they want the same thing as you. They fail to mention they likely won't want it for at least another ten years.

- People in the normal range will originally have long interesting cultural conversations, and later will spend much more time on the couch watching TV.

- Misrepresenters will check the "looking for a relationship" box on their online dating profiles. They just don't tell you they want to date a million women until they find their Princess – your chances of fulfilling his fantasy are next to nil.

- People in the normal range will not eat gassy foods at first, but then later bring on the beans and broccoli.

- And my favourite: misrepresenters will refrain from bringing up their serious commitment issues until they've slept with you. Once that notch in the bedpost has been firmly chiselled, they can't wait to tell you why they're not available.

I remember as if they were yesterday, waking up with the hot hunk from the night before who wasted no time telling me, "I have some data to share with you."

Lizard Brain: "Data!! He's got some data. It can't be good. Run. Run!"

And then, out it shot from his mouth. "I have a girlfriend."

Ahhh, she's the data. I see. Well, that would have been good to know yesterday!

The confusing part was that he and I had met a few weeks before and spent quite a bit of time together organizing a local event. At no point was data around or even mentioned!

"Yes, she's working out of town," he murmurs awkwardly from the other side of the grand chasm that has split the bed in two.

Ahhh, yes. The data works out of town. Hmmmm. Did the data really exist? I don't know. I didn't care. I was done. The alarms really went off when he referred to the other woman as "some data." It takes a little of the romance out of it all.

Another fellow said all the right things: "I haven't felt like this in such a long time, I feel so connected to you." Such a gentleman, this guy waited until after the second time we slept together to say, "My heart just isn't available."

After that I insisted on having a heartfelt conversation with my dates, and quickly said my goodbyes if it was clear that I was not going to get any straight answers.

If you are getting confusing messages, the best option is to say: "I care about you and would like to continue to date you, but I'm looking for a monogamous, long-term relationship," or "I'd really like to be married and have children within the next three years," or "If we're not on the same page, I can't continue going out with you, but if you do decide you want the same thing, look me up."

Be ready to say it and be sure you mean it.

If he's ready, and you are what he wants, he'll come after you. He's more likely to figure it out by missing you, rather than you turning yourself into a pretzel in order to stay with him.

As I was learning about clearly articulating my needs, I had an opportunity to practise when Jeff, the fellow I was dating said, "I'm not really looking for a long-term relationship right now."

I said, "Okay, I understand. That's too bad because I really like you, but I am looking for a long-term, monogamous commitment. I wish you well."

This wasn't said as a threat. I said it because I meant it. I was willing to walk away so we could both find what we were looking for. I didn't realize at the time that I was about to find out where he really stood.

He came back and we went on to have a three-year relationship. In the end we decided it wasn't right, but that initial interaction changed our dynamic. I could have continued to date him casually, hoping that he would change, but I had already been down that road too many times before.

It's easy to point the finger and say, "He's always playing the non-commitment game with me." This is where the rubber meets the road and where the power lies with you to make changes, to start to get on your own page to happiness. It's much harder to ask yourself, "How can I ask for what I want? And am I willing to walk away if our long term goals are not compatible??"

Doing everything his way without asking for what you want is only going to make you both unhappy in the long run. Learning how to draw your line in the sand is another essential step.

CHAPTER 10

Trading In The Pumpkin For A
More Reliable Vehicle

The blissful, lusty, hormonally charged beginning of a relationship that feels like "falling in love" is something that just happens. But what about when the magic dust wears off? You then face the task of seeing whether or not the two of you really fit.

I met Rick on the Internet. He was a solid guy with no mixed messages, which was a great start. When he told me he had been married for thirty years and was serious about being married again I knew I had met a long-term guy. I liked him. He was reliable with values I admired and he considered my needs and desires.

We had lots in common, but when I started to become acquainted with his friends, the picture shifted. Rick was a sailor, and most sailors have a reputation for being hard drinking. He lived on his yacht at a local sailing club and there was usually a group of people hoisting a few on any given night.

After going to several outings with his friends, I realized this just wasn't my scene. I used to be a party girl and could knock back a few with the best of them, but being the only sober person in a drinking crowd is no fun for me at all.

Time to check in.

"Rick, I feel quite uncomfortable when you and your friends are drinking. It doesn't appeal to me anymore and I don't like being around people who are drunk. I can't relate to what is going on."

His response was "Are you telling me I drink too much?"

"No, I'm not talking about you. I'm talking about me. I'm saying that I don't like to drink anymore and I don't like to be around people who are drinking."

"Oh, well, we'll just have to go shopping around to find you a drink you like, maybe a nice light wine. You'll enjoy that."

"No, that's not what I'm saying. I like the taste of many kinds of drinks, I just don't like the effect it has on me and I don't like to drink anymore. I also find it hard to talk to people who are drunk."

This went back and forth a few more times. I'm not sure if he ever understood.

Our interaction gave me some information. Not only are we not on the same page about drinking, I knew I could expect tough conversations whenever there was a difference between us.

I continued to share and check in with him as time went on, but found I was enjoying myself less and less when we were together.

He told me he got turned off when what I shared with him didn't match what he wanted. I felt like I was stuck in his fantasy and he couldn't see who I really was even when I was telling him point blank. It was like being stuck into a shoe that was the wrong size.

As much as I liked and admired Rick, we didn't last more than a few months. The old me would have hung in there for a couple of years before I stopped trying to hammer us into a mould we didn't fit.

Eddie, on the other hand, celebrates and participates in my check-ins. This brings us closer. It's great to know that we want the same things and are heading in the same direction.

Rick and I remained on friendly terms. Since breaking up we have each gone on to find love and marriage. We found partners that matched us rather than trying to cram ourselves into someone else's fantasy.

Your Relationship: Toddling It To Adulthood

Consider that your relationship is like a child. You and your partner are the parents, and depending on the age of the relationship, you need to provide age-appropriate attention and nurturing for the romance to grow strong and healthy. Seeing your relationship as a child means that you can't expect a very young partnership to know how to provide for your needs. But like a baby, your new involvement is all-consuming. You spend a lot of time getting to know each other. Yet if your relationship is only a couple of months old, assume that you will be providing a lot of guidance in the form of talking and sharing who you are and what's important to you.

A year in, the relationship should be able to stumble around and has some legs of its own to stand on. Little ones need to know what the guidelines are. That way they don't get hurt.

Ongoing lines in the sand need to be drawn – we'll go into more detail about those.

At age two you can rely on a blooming independence that can provide more depth where it didn't exist before. The child is now learning to talk and communicate more effectively, some misunderstandings about boundaries still happen, but mistakes are considered tools for learning.

At age five you have a being that can fully communicate and continues to learn and grow. You still need to pay attention to what's going on, but it can get around independently and has a life of its own.

By age eighteen, the groundwork is laid. You have a fully contributing adult that still needs to be treated with love, yet can offer much in return.

Looking at a relationship like a child reminds us that a love relationship is active, alive and responsive, not passive. Each partner is responsible for contributing to the health and welfare of the relationship. If you are finding yourself constantly upset, it's time to check in. You need to see if what you are expecting the relationship to provide is age appropriate. Let's take a look at how other couples have dealt with their relationship challenges.

CHAPTER 11

Drawing A Line In The Sandcastle

After some deep soul searching Sally is considering breaking off her ten-year relationship with Wayne. "We have a lot of fun, a lot in common and get along really well when we're together," she says.

"The issue for me is when we get closer and start to feel more emotionally intimate, he leaves. Suddenly I'll get a text saying, "I'm in Los Angeles and I'll be back in two weeks." It would be the first I time I had heard about him going out of town. Or we'll have dinner plans and he no-shows."

Sally starts to speak through her tears. "I have been waiting for what seems like forever to have our relationship go to the next step, but after ten years, we're still playing this here-one-day-gone-the-next game and I'm tired of it. I don't know if there is something I'm doing to push him away, but I'm willing to get some help to find out."

We humans are a very tough species. It can sometimes take years for us to get tired of our pain. Resilient as we are, the good news is that pain is a pointer saying something is stealing our happiness. At this point we become willing to stop enduring pain and find a healthy solution. We have to start aiming the arrow in the direction we really want.

Up until now Wayne has had no reason to change and probably doesn't see any problems with the relationship the way it is. Sally has not yet told him that she wants more from their relationship. She is now ready for a closer bond.

It would be easy to see Wayne as the unreliable, heart-breaking cad, yet Sally has been playing the part of victim to the here-today-gone-tomorrow lover. Her pattern was to continue to take him back without question as soon as he landed on her doorstep.

In another woman's case, a relationship like this might work. She may be happy with the relationship the way it is. If it works for both people, there's nothing to change.

For Sally it wasn't okay. The casual quality of the relationship was causing her too much pain and she now felt ready to draw a line in the sand.

After some counselling help, Sally shared her needs with Wayne and let him know how his running away affected her. "Every time we start to get emotionally close, it feels like you rip yourself away and leave. That is very painful for me. I want something else from our relationship. I want a dynamic where both of us can share our fears and will stay to work it out rather than run away when things feel scary or uncomfortable. I want a long-term commitment from a man and I would really like that man to be you."

He said he wanted the same thing.

How great is that? She asks for her needs to be met and he agrees without question.

Sadly, that wasn't where it ended.

"We tried for a while and nothing changed. He even came to counselling with me a few times. When he got uncomfortable, I would ask him to stay and he could never pull it off. After a few months of trying, I told him if he didn't stay the next time, I would end the relationship because it was too painful for me. I realized that once I said this, there would be no going back. I needed to know how willing he was, and I knew I would risk losing the relationship."

"What he did next shocked me: he proposed! He had heard that I wanted him to show me how serious he was and this was his way of proving it. I couldn't believe it. I was thrilled, as I had wanted this for years. Happy as I was, a niggling thought in the back of my head said, 'Is this going to change things?' I didn't know what to do and went to my counsellor for advice. His words were helpful, but painful to hear."

"This man is offering you a crumb. Don't mistake it for a loaf."

"It was the hardest thing I had ever heard. I spent the next two days holed up in my apartment, crying my eyes out. I let ten years worth of pain and tears come gushing out. At the end I got up and dusted myself off. I was clear that I had to stick to what I had originally said. Being married wouldn't make any difference if he kept leaving all the time. I needed to know he would stay when the going got tough. I put the proposal on hold and remained firm. We tried a few more times, but he never could stay. I broke off the relationship."

Sally said, "I was still in love with this man and had spent ten years of my life with him, yet I am more committed to my own happiness than a lifetime of heartbreak. In the moments when I am missing him badly and feel like reaching out to him, I turn to my friends and counsellor for help instead. It wasn't easy, but it was more important not to give up on myself so I can finally find the love I want."

For ten years Sally had put up with Wayne's in and out behaviour. By tolerating it and not expressing her needs she had ten years of heartbreak.

Sally's drawing a line in the sand was similar to my experience with Jeff, a guy I dated who said he didn't want a serious relationship. Things would have gone very differently if I had continued to date him without expressing my own desire for a long-term, monogamous commitment. I was willing to walk away when he said he didn't want the same thing. I know he did the I-don't-want-a-commitment dance with other women after he and I had split up and would have done the same with me if I hadn't articulated my own needs.

A few months into our marriage, I noticed Eddie becoming critical of me, which was out of character for the kind, happy-go-lucky guy he is. How did we get here? I realized he was mirroring how I had been treating him. I was repeating my family pattern of using criticism as a way to get what you want. This old behaviour pattern kept me in my familiar comfort zone, rather than risking raising the level of my love-o-meter. I knew I wanted something different in my marriage, so it was time for me to draw a line in the sand on my own behaviour. I didn't want to affect my marriage this way.

I told Eddie what I had noticed and promised I would try to stop myself before becoming critical with him. I explained that it wasn't what I wanted for us, that I wanted to be kind and loving toward each other and he agreed. I was determined to establish loving patterns for our marriage and Eddie got it. I had the power to create something different by being different.

Who Parked My Pumpkin?

Eddie is a creature of habit who likes life to follow a routine. I, however, like variety and don't have anything in my life that I would call routine. It's rare that anything happens twice the same way for me.

And so began our marriage. At first everything was over the top crazy, love stuff, but not long after the I do's and the move in together, Eddie settled easily into the old comfy slippers of his life, while I started to go stir crazy. I wanted to get into my glass slippers and go out dancing. I love to socialize and entertain but was too embarrassed to have friends over to our impenetrable apartment. The lime green plastic covered couch may as well have been a moat around our old, worn out castle. Our sex life had too quickly turned into if-this-is-Saturday-it-must-be-sex-night. After a few months I started to panic. I was feeling emotionally disconnected from Eddie and when he approached me for sex, I felt guarded and unable to open up sexually to him.

I tried what I knew: I asked for what I wanted. I repeated it to make sure it landed. Still nothing was happening. I got more frustrated every day and as I found myself shutting down I was beginning to think my marriage was doomed.

One day at a Clearmind workshop, my teacher Catherine discovered me blowing my nose loudly. "Are you sick?"

I answered back with a nasal, snot-filled wail, "No, I'm crying."

Not one of my better moments.

I told her the whole sordid story and she quietly responded, "You have to give what you want to get." Catherine has a canny way of switching on light bulbs and this time it really lit up the dark places. What she was saying was similar to teaching someone how to treat you. By giving Eddie what I wanted to get, I was showing him what I wanted.

Lizard Brain: Duh!!

I thought my job was to ask for what I wanted and then sit and wait to see what he came up with. It was a blind spot for me to be an example of what I wanted. Again, it was time for me to draw a line in the sand on myself, pull up my big girl panties and try something new.

So, that night, I went home and as it got close to bed time, I lit some candles in the bedroom, put on some slinky music, changed into something a little more comfortable...and guess what? Routine guy never showed up that evening and it felt like we were on our honeymoon again.

Since I was on a roll, I decided to fulfil my desire for more social/friend time. I rented a cabin at Manning Park and invited some friends to come for the weekend. I arranged all the food and we took turns preparing it. We canoed, swam, threw a ball around, played hacky sack, and shot pool and threw darts at the pub. It was lots of fun and made me realize that I may not have a home where people can come to socialize, but that doesn't stop me from creating a place where we can congregate. It just takes a little ingenuity, which makes it even more fun.

Drawing my own line in the sand gives me more control over my life and my marriage and I can create what I do want and say, "No" to what I don't.

How To Talk So Prince Charming Can Hear You

My ex-roommate Karen was a master at having men turn to putty in her hands. Not only was she in a happy, steady relationship but at work she was the manager of eighty men who respected her. Karen is very to the point. "I direct the men by telling them what I want, by when and they do it. Everything I ask from them meets their objectives and makes their jobs run more smoothly, which makes it easy for them to be on board. With new people I give more explanation so they can understand the purpose I have in mind for a given project. Seasoned vets trust me and are happy doing what I ask. It's very different from the way I would communicate with women. These guys aren't interested in small talk or emotions or long drawn out sagas. They just want to know what to do, why they are doing it and then they do it. It works for me both in and out of intimate relationships."

Karen told me: "When I fell into my current relationship, I wasn't looking for love. I wasn't desperate or needy and didn't cling to John, nor did I date him exclusively for more than a year. I was just happy to spend time with him and have fun. That worked well for both of us. And yet, we would often run into each other strictly by chance. I would be grocery shopping, or out with friends, or driving along the street, and voila! There he was. The Universe just kept putting him in front of me."

When Karen told me this, it really struck a chord, as I was interested in a guy who lived two minutes away from me. He had to walk past my front door regularly and yet I never ran into him even once by chance – not once. Looking back, I see the Universe was helping me out too as it turned out he wasn't a good match for me.

Karen was great at telling John what worked for her and what didn't. "One time John threw a burning cigarette butt into the bushes by my house. I was appalled, not only because I don't want to live around stinky cigarette butts, but it could have started a fire. I asked him not to do that again."

John said, "I don't need my girl telling me what to do."

Karen said, "No you don't, but if you behave like that again, I won't be your girl."

"I explained why it was important to me and he realized I really meant it. He never did that again."

Karen cared about John, but not enough to be willing to compromise her values.

As she shared her story I stood there with my mouth open. My brain circuits were zapping all over the place. Never in a million years would I have been that direct. A few years down the road and many, many counselling sessions later, I know that if a man wants me to compromise who I am to suit him, then he really isn't the guy for me.

Counselling Mind: It is not what others do that is the cause of our struggle. When we allow someone to step over our line in the sand without saying anything, we are giving up on ourselves and setting ourselves up for more pain. If you never stand up and tell people when something affects you in a way you don't like, they have no way of knowing.

Karen never seemed to be in pain with John because her boundaries were clear and she wasn't looking for any Prince Charming. She accepted John for who he was. One night she came home earlier than expected. "John and his friends were getting really drunk and I wasn't enjoying myself. I was happy to come home to get a few things done. So I kissed him good-night and left."

Huh? I would never have done that.

"I don't blame John for the way he spends his time. I'm content to do my own thing if the way we want to spend time doesn't match. Sometimes he'll really want me to stay, so we'll find something that we both want to do, otherwise he understands why I decide to leave."

If this had been me, I would have whined or seethed and made him the bad guy for doing what he wanted instead of paying attention to me. I would have told myself that he didn't care about me as much as he cared about his friends. It would never have occurred to me to draw my own line in the sand and say, "I love you, but I'm not having fun so I'm going to leave." Never in a million years.

After learning some how-to-treat-a-guy tips from Karen, I started applying them to my relationship with my new date, Paul. More than a few times when we were out socially and I wasn't having fun, I knew I had a choice. I didn't always choose to leave, but knew I could at any time which made me feel freer and more independent. I now had a new tool that I could draw a line in the sand or wipe it out at any time.

I didn't need to make Paul a bad guy for being who he is and enjoying the kind of fun he does. Instead I had an inner litmus test to see if we had enough in common. What I found was that I was having less and less fun being with him, which told me he really wasn't the guy for me.

The New Improved List

It's unlikely that I could ever be as detached as Karen. She and I are very different in that way. Watching her, however, helped me to make some different choices. In addition to the am-I-having-fun query, Karen taught me to ask other important questions when I was dating. The imperative thing to note is that these are questions you are asking yourself. Notice these questions are mostly about you.

This became my new List:

- Do I feel attracted to this man and do we have fun together?

- Is he physically, mentally and emotionally available for a relationship? Am I getting mixed messages?

- Am I really ready and available? Am I sending mixed messages?

- Can I talk to him about an uncomfortable topic or something that I think is important?

- Do we share my most important values?

- How do I feel when I'm with this person? How do I feel when we're not together?

- Does being with this man enhance my life?

- And, the most important question of all, and one that I will be forever grateful to Karen for: Do I feel that this person has my best interests at heart?

The best part is that when I moved out of Karen's place, John moved in. After dating for three years, they realized how well their relationship worked, and decided to take the next step.

It's one thing when someone else's behaviour affects us in ways we don't like, but what happens when we need to draw a line in the sand about our own behaviour? Shopping, sugar binging, drinking to destruction? Where do we say no to what isn't making our partners or us truly happy? Or what if, like Amy, we are helping our partner in behaviour we don't really like?

"When my husband gets home from work, he expects me to have a triple scotch on the rocks ready to put in his hand after he takes his coat off. I make it without question, but even as I'm pouring it, I start to feel sick to my stomach as I know it's likely to be the first of a few and I'm going to end up with a slurring lump of a husband on the couch for the rest of the evening. I'm grateful he's not a nasty drunk; he doesn't beat me or get mean. He just gets slower and slower until he falls asleep on the couch and I drag him into bed later."

Lizard Brain: Wow! That's sounds like fun!

Amy defends. "Oh, on the weekends we'll invite his friends from work over, so I throw together some snacks and we socialize and have fun. I enjoy it until everyone starts to get drunk, then I just go to bed. I don't think anyone notices that I've left."

Counselling Mind: Are you happy?

"Yes, I'm pretty happy." But her eyes betray her. Not even a hint of a smile comes on her face.

Perhaps one day Amy will realize that she deserves more in life and that she doesn't need to live with this pain. Then she will draw a line in the sand for herself and her husband.

Amy's case shows how over-functioning creates exactly what she doesn't want. But there's more to this dynamic. By not telling her husband that she doesn't like him getting drunk every night, not only is she not being clear about what she wants, she is also depriving him of the opportunity to see how his behaviour is affecting her happiness and their relationship. He has no reason to think his behaviour is not OK with her. When she hasn't shared the information, he isn't being given a choice to do something different.

Counselling Mind: You're not doing either you or your mate any favours by letting these crippling situations slide. When we tell them the effect of their behaviour, they get to face their feelings and the consequences of their actions. Taking away their struggle means they lose the opportunity to learn and grow.

Another way of over-functioning is, like Alice, trying to change your partner's behaviour so that you don't have to feel your own discomfort.

"I used to tell my husband what he should and shouldn't say on the way to meeting my work colleagues: 'Now don't just say you're in plumbing. Tell them you own your own plumbing business so that it looks better. And please make sure you don't mention that we have live-in students to help with the bills.'"

Alice is dumping her fear about being judged by her peers onto her husband, and he is getting the message that she doesn't trust him to use his own discretion. She needs to see that at the heart of her embarrassment is shame about her life. Trying to control her husband is her way of hiding from what she feels. For Alice to grow she would have to face her own insecurities including allowing him to say what he wants to say.

You're Gettin' What You're Teachin'

In the movie, *The Break Up,* Jennifer Aniston and Vince Vaughn are a couple who are splitting up but are still living together while they sell their condo.

As she's packing, he says, "I don't want us to break up."

She snivels through tears, "I was always the one that made all the effort. I folded your socks, I cooked your dinner, and

I made all of our social plans. I really made an effort for this relationship and you never made any. I never felt like you respected or appreciated me or anything I did."

He says, "You've never said this before."

"I have in subtle ways."

"You may think you have hinted at these things before, but I don't understand hints. You have to tell me directly. I'm not a mind reader."

Jennifer's plea is the typical cry of the caretaker/over-functioner type. By doing everything, she has created a dependent man. Confusingly, she then gets mad at him for not contributing more. She sees him as lazy, yet she did her part to create the situation in the first place. It took an honest conversation between them to throw light on the dysfunction of the relationship and there is now an opportunity for both of them to do something different.

People treat you the way you teach them to. Although it may seem like a contradiction to love, tolerating unhealthy behaviour is not a loving act for you or your partner. A line in the sand means you care enough to want to make a difference to the relationship.

When someone's behaviour affects you in a way that doesn't work for you, then drawing a line in the sand means you are taking a stand for yourself – your values, your needs and your desires. As you explore where this line is for you and then share it with others with both of your best interests in mind, your love-o-meter goes up a notch and you become a better partner for your mate, a better daughter and a better friend to the people you care about.

Drawing a line in the sand on your own over-functioning allows your partner to make his own mistakes, struggle through his own hardships and feel his own feelings, which then allows him to grow his love-o-meter.

Counselling Mind: One thing to note – much talk is thrown around these days about establishing boundaries. Drawing a line in the sand is a bit different. Boundaries can be all about someone else and what they are doing wrong. Lines in the sand come from your heart. They are an exploration of yourself and what you want to create in your life. Boundaries can be made with a sense of defence, which is based on fear. Lines in the sand are based on doing what is a loving act, for both you and your mate. They can show you where you may be crossing a line that isn't healthy and can do the same for your partner.

There is an African tribe that does the most beautiful thing that is a perfect example of a line in the sand: when someone does something hurtful to another, they take the person to the centre of town, and the entire tribe comes and surrounds them. For two days they'll tell the person every good thing he or she has ever done. The tribe believes that every human being comes into the world as good, each of us desiring safety, love, peace and happiness. Sometimes in the pursuit of those things people make mistakes. The community sees misdeeds as a cry for help. They band together for the sake of their fellow man to hold him up, to reconnect him with his true nature, to remind him who he really is, until he remembers the truth from which he'd temporarily been disconnected: "I am good."

This is a world away from the culture that most of the rest of the planet has cultivated. Yet, if you search your heart, does this idea not touch something within you?

It's easy to understand all of these ideas as concepts, and even to start putting them into practice. Talking to your mate from a loving place about how you would like to move forward and inviting them to come with you. Reminding each other that we are good people and that sometimes we just make mistakes or lose our way. But what about those moments when you feel so crazy angry and more than any-thing, you want to cross that line in the sand and just lash out. Then what do you do?

CHAPTER 12

Calming The Emotional Storm

A male friend once complained, "You women are too emotional. You complicate everything and get upset at the silliest things."

"Yeah," my quick-witted girlfriend responded, "you think it's hard on your end. Try being me!"

In the DVD, *A Tale of Two Brains,* national marriage expert Mark Gungor explains how a woman's brain is a very complex organ that is a multi-tasking, multi-dimensional superhighway. He says, "Women care about everything!"

For me, this is not an issue, but for my male friend it definitely was. I realize it's not the fact that women have emotions that men see as the problem but the way they express them when they are upset.

As mentioned in the last chapter, taking a stand for your needs and desires is an important step in learning how to create a new dynamic in a relationship. Another essential aspect in keeping a relationship happy and healthy is learning what to do when you get emotionally upset.

A counsellor might prescribe calling a time-out and coming back to talk about your issue when you have both cooled down. That's a good step, but there is an even richer way that brings greater insight into what hides beneath the upset in the first place.

A Course in Miracles states that you are never upset for the reason you think. It's a bit of a mind bender, but the more I explore the roadmap of my emotional make up and psyche, it holds true. If we can get beyond our defence systems to what is really going on, we discover levels of blame and shame and disconnect. Clearmind taught me a process that can take me from extreme anger to peaceful calm in twenty minutes. It takes us through the layers of our psyche to what is underneath our blame and shame and reveals the unconscious belief that is causing so much upset. Without fail, what is unveiled at the end of the process is never what I was angry about in the first place. Once we get to know ourselves, we can share these layers with the people we care about and it becomes an invitation to a deeper intimacy and connection with our partners and ourselves.

Case in point:

Eddie told me his old friends were coming to town. One of them was playing at a bar in a hard rock cover band with the rest of the old gang there to watch and party. I knew these guys when they were young and I didn't trust them. The fact that they were still hanging around bars and playing in hard rock cover bands told me, at forty-five, they were still rough and tumble teenagers at heart.

Immediately my gut started churning and I wanted to yell, "Nooooo!" with every cell of my being. Too often in the past a partner had gone out partying and I didn't feel like our relationship was being respected around other women. This made me extremely tense and angry. Now having explored my own emotional upsets and reactions, I knew there was something underneath that I could share with Eddie. So, instead going with my initial impulse of yelling and telling him that he and his friends were immature and disrespectful, I took a deep breath and calmly asked him, "Are you going?"

"Well, I'd like to catch up with my friends, but hanging out in a bar with everyone getting pissed out of their minds watching a hard rock cover band doesn't really appeal to me. I think I'll skip it."

I was glad I hadn't let my emotions take over.

The night of the show as we were lying in bed together, he casually mentioned, "My buddies' band is probably playing right now." That got my gut churning again. My idea of love doesn't include old friends chasing women and acting like single teenagers on the make. Usually my insecurity runs the show and I try to criticize and manipulate my partner so he will feel insecure and it would create a false sense of safety for me.

Instead, I shared what I was feeling: "My guts are churning at the very idea of you going out with those guys. I've had lots of boyfriends who got a big ego boost by flirting with other women. I felt unwanted and invisible. It's not that I want to change you, but the whole situation was bringing up a lot of insecurity for me."

This was what my training taught me to do: share the feelings that were lurking behind my automatic reaction and then look for the belief that lies behind the feelings. "I'm afraid you're going to get bored with me, that you will find someone more interesting and attractive and I will lose you and end up alone." I was inviting Eddie to come deeper and deeper into my psyche and my emotional world.

"Bunny, I don't need or want other women to boost my ego and the most important thing in the world to me is right there," he said pointing to our marriage licence that hangs on the wall by his pillow. Where I used to see betrayal and rejection, all I could feel now was love.

I've drawn my husband closer by letting him see my vulnerability rather than making him the bad guy when I feel insecure. Eddie's love and understanding tells me a ton about who he is. He could have reacted and told me what an insecure, snivelling sop I was. But he didn't. He treated me with great care and love, reassuring me about how he really feels. It's in these moments that I realize he has my best interests at heart.

This makes the lime green plastic on my couch worth it.

Counselling Mind: It's not your partner's job to fill up your love-o-meter. It's your job to find the path to reassurance by sharing your feelings and beliefs and, when needed, reaching out for help. In fact, it's impossible for him or anyone else but you. This is what grows the level in your love-o-meter.

This exchange with Eddie helped me define what was once a fuzzy line in the sand when it comes to monogamous relationships. It's not just "Don't sleep with someone else," it's also any behaviour that suggests, "Hey, I think you're hot and if I wasn't already tied down, I'd be all over you."

When I didn't know how to draw a line in the sand or share my fears and insecurities, I just got mad and pointed the finger at my boyfriend. After ranting on and on about what a bad person he was, he would chalk me up as just another jealous girlfriend. He didn't take me seriously. How could he?

By sharing your line in the sand in an open, loving way that invites connection, you will soon see how ready for real intimacy your partner is. If he treats you with kindness when you share your vulnerabilities, you know you have a keeper!

Mr. Tidbit

Cathy is used to living with Mr. Tidbit. Like her Dad, her partner only gives her tidbits of time, tidbits of love, tidbits of sincerity. "He would do the same thing my Dad did. Even when we were together, he barely spoke to me. He would promise something and I would get my hopes up. Then he didn't carry through with it. Staying late at the office or heading to the pub with his buddies always took priority over spending time with me."

Taking a journey of self-discovery changed everything for her. "In the past I got really angry and blamed the man in my life for not living up to my expectations and desires. I discovered the hidden belief that my emotions are too much for a man. So the less he is around, the less chance I have of being too much for him: too emotional, too angry and too scary. Maybe it's better if I only see him in little bits, so I don't scare him away."

"My pattern was to choose men that only gave me tidbits of time and then I got angry at them for doing so. When I met Steve, I wanted to take a step toward creating a new and healthier relationship than hanging around with Mr. Tidbit. So instead of being angry with him when I was upset, I would go and hit pillows in private. Later I would talk to him about my feelings. I felt sad but hopeful, so that's what I shared with him: 'I really like you. I'd like a closer intimate relationship where we spend more time together. I'd like that someone to be you. Do you want that too?'"

He didn't.

"I was heartbroken. It was really hard for me to walk away because it felt as though my heart was being ripped out. I so wanted to just go back into my old pattern of putting up with the tidbits, but I also knew that I wouldn't be happy living that lie. A few midnight movies and a many boxes of tissue later, I was feeling better. I missed Mr. Tidbit but knew in my heart I am much more committed to finding the love I really want."

Counselling Mind: The idea I'd like to plant is that there is a journey to be undertaken, a new path to clear through the unseen beliefs that you don't even know are lurking in the undergrowth of the subconscious. You can't do it on your own. Like having a blindfold on with no way to remove it and yet still hoping to be able to see, you need a guide to lead you down the twisty trails of your psyche.

The Emotional Lock And Key

In the movie, *What the Bleep,* Candice Pert claims that we have what she calls a lock and key system in our bodies that unlocks our emotions. If we have a sudden rush of anger, there will be little keys created in that moment that rush from all parts of our bodies to find the little locks hidden in our cells that relate to anger. There are keys for every emotion and only the angry keys lock into the sad locks. When our cells divide, it creates multiples of whichever lock the cell holds, so if you feel angry a lot, your cells will create more and more angry locks. If, on the other hand, you start to do more and more things that make you happy, your cells will divide into more and more happy locks, so there will be lots of places for the happy keys to find when they are looking for a place to land.

It's a great idea to practise the new skills of unravelling your emotional layers with other like-minded people. In group therapy, safety is the top priority and you will soon discover that beneath all the layers of attack and guilt we are all the same. By working together you learn from each other's situation; sharing allows you to see that we all have blind spots.

When I shared my fear about Eddie hanging out with old buddies in a bar, the other women in my therapy group shared how they also felt disrespected when their partners flirted with other women. Then the men shared. Some men said their partners were saying the same thing, but they really didn't understand what they were talking about. All they knew was that their wives were upset. Talking about it in a group shed light on what the blind spot was for the men. They didn't realize they were crossing the line between fun and flirting. The last thing they wanted was that their wives felt unloved and disrespected. They resolved to explore the beliefs that were unconsciously driving this behaviour. The women in the room, including me, discovered that there was no hurtful intent – just blind spots. Understanding this makes me treat my partner with more compassion and less reaction.

Learning about how my emotions work and how they are controlled by my unconscious beliefs shows me how it colours what I think about other people. My brain automatically makes up scenarios based on these beliefs and then they create my emotions. For example, I was convinced that a co-worker of mine hated me. She seemed distant and rarely spoke to me. I felt resentful and decided to not even bother trying to get closer to her. Over time, and learning to question my beliefs, I noticed that she wasn't singling me out; she was simply shy and more introverted than I am.

Counselling has allowed me to turn around my unconscious beliefs and have more compassion and understanding for other people. One day I felt a sense of empathy for her and, as I did with Eddie, told her what was really underneath my judgement of her. I let her know why I avoided her and what I had discovered. She then told me more about herself, which automatically brought us closer. Since then we often laugh about our old situation and are becoming closer every day.

As I learn about the roadmap of my emotions, the more Candice Pert's theory makes sense. I realized there was much more to meditation, relaxation and doing the things in life that inspire and motivate me. The more often I tap into a place of relaxation and peacefulness, the more I create peaceful keys and more peaceful locks for my keys to find. Our body is a pattern-making machine. It's going to build more locks and keys whether we guide the process or not, so we may as well help our body go in the direction we want.

Another way to look at it is this. You have a thought in your brain every 1.2 seconds, that is sixty- to eighty-thousand per day. When you have a thought that means nothing to you, you won't even notice it. When a thought comes into your brain that means something to you, it will have a specific pathway in your brain that has been etched in from past programming, like a groove in a record. When that thought attaches to that pathway, the pathway leads to a feeling that creates your keys. When your keys fit into your locks, it becomes an emotion, which then drives your behaviour. You cry, you yell at someone, you eat an entire container of Ben and Jerry's ice cream, or you go shopping and spend your rent money.

Now when I'm noticing an emotional state coming on that I don't like or isn't productive, I take a new step. I could just relax in that moment, which will help my body and brain reprogram itself, which in itself is progress in the direction I want to go. But since I am on a spiritual path, I take it one step further and it's the one step that makes a world of difference. I surrender my problem or my emotional state over to my higher power. Instead of having to know what to do or find a solution, I trust that my higher power will have the best solution with my best interests at heart. Sometimes it requires feeling some very uncomfortable feelings, and it always requires time and patience as I wait for the answer, but I am never disappointed.

Meditate, dance around the room, eat what your body likes, exercise, surrender a problem or emotion to your higher power or do something you enjoy and find fulfilling. Science is now proving the more you do things that help you to feel peaceful and happy, the easier it becomes to feel peaceful and happy. Who wouldn't want that?

Last but not least, I encourage people to find a way to help them discover their own personal road map of their emotional body. Emotions govern a great deal of our lives, but how much do we actually know about them, or more importantly, how to have a different relationship to them when they are sabotaging what we really want. I'll talk a little more about this near the end of the book.

CHAPTER 13

Asking The Tough Questions

There are two ways to check in to see if you are thinking straight about a relationship. One way is to check in with yourself and ask some tough questions. Sometimes you need to ask the questions of the person you are dating.

If you are in dating pain and want to have a good long talk with yourself, there are some key questions you may want to ponder.

Sheila, who was dating Mr. Future Promise, was surprised by what she found after she asked herself these questions:

- What is the **Cinderella fantasy** I have of this situation/ relationship? What am I holding out for that I hope will change?

- What is the reality? What is happening right now?

- If this man is going to be the same for the rest of his life as he is today, can I live with that?

- Is he willing and capable of working together to make changes? Am I?

- How much am I expecting the relationship to nurture me rather than me bringing what I want into the relationship?

Sheila says, "The promise is clear. I got caught up in the fantasy he has in his head about being rich and hobnobbing all over the world. He says we're going to go to Bali together and says he'll stop drinking and start working out. I started seeing him as the man of my dreams."

"But when I check in I see that none of that is even close to real. The truth is that he is getting kicked out of his apartment because he can't pay the rent. The stress of losing his apartment has him drinking even more and of course he can't afford gym membership fees."

"I asked him if he was willing to make some changes. He says yes, but he has been saying that for months and still nothing changes. If nothing is going to change, then no, I don't want to be with him for the rest of my life."

"Looking back, I've been expecting the relationship to be my saviour rather than bringing what I want to it. To be honest, I'm really not feeling attracted enough to him to put in the effort. He seems more like my big brother than someone I want to continue to explore a relationship with."

Sometimes if the relationship is important, it is worth your while to make changes. Sometimes, like Sheila, the questions make it clear that you're not willing to continue the relationship. Either way, you can start to move on rather than stay stuck in a situation you don't want.

For Gail, still pining seven years after her man has left her, the check-in questions brought her the clarity she needed to break free of the emotional pain she was hanging on to.

"In my fantasy he suddenly shows up on my doorstep, tells me he was wrong and he is sorry and that he's been thinking about me every moment. He knows that he loves me madly and wants me to be his wife and we will live happily together forever."

"The reality was that when he was around everything was on his terms and he only came over twice a week. As long as I never tried to contact him or ask for more, all was well. Looking back I had a sense that I should never bring up the topic of wanting more in our relationship. In truth, he never made any commitment to me at all. When I asked him to come to a friend's wedding, he walked out and hasn't made any contact in seven years. When I think about it, his reaction seems extreme. If he didn't want to go, all he had to say was 'No.'"

"If things were never to change from the way it was, only seeing him for dinner twice a week, then no, I wouldn't want the relationship. If he had been willing to work on it with me, he would still be here today. We had a lot of fun while he was around, but I want a long-term committed relationship. Next time I'll check in and ask a few questions much earlier. Maybe he did me a favour by never coming back."

Lizard Brain: Yeah, Gail! You really got it!

If you are still regretting the end of a relationship, I would encourage you to get out a notebook and ask these questions for yourself. They will help get your feet back on the ground and see where you have been lost in the *Cinderella Fantasy*.

When dating Mixed Message Joe, the check-in questions helped me get clarity when faced with his I-really-like-you-but-I-want-to-date-other-women dance. I asked Joe a direct question that left no holes for misinterpretation.

"I'm wondering if you are ready to pursue a one-on-one rela- tionship, and are willing to do that with me?"

Perhaps because I asked a direct and simple question, Joe was finally able to respond clearly. He said, "No."

When I asked him point blank, I was able to see that he was never serious about me. I was glad I didn't spend any more time continuing to date him, hoping he would fall in love when it was now clear that he had no intention to do so and just wanted to play the field.

If he had responded with more mixed messages, I was ready to stand firm and not be pulled back into the warm and fuzzy fantasy I had so wanted to believe in.

Don't Believe Everything You Think

Our brains are meaning-making machines. Whenever we see a situation, we make a conclusion about it. That conclusion is, in fact, an assumption and may not reflect reality at all. When your brain sees either an Ogre or Prince Charming, watch out! It's time for a check in.

Eddie and I have a jar of change we collect for nights we want to go out for dinner or order in. Given Eddie's diet of hot dogs, hamburgers and pizza, I feel constrained by his choices and noticed I was starting to rebel. My preference is Asian or some kind of ethnic food. I was having a particu- larly harried moment (read hissy fit) about it when a friend offered an idea, "My husband and I often order from two dif- ferent places."

"Huh?" Zip zap brain circuits. My first thoughts were:

- But that would cost more money.

- Big Bad Ogre Eddie would fight me on doing it that way because he won't change his eating pattern and he wouldn't want my eating habits to cost more.

- I can't ask for something for myself. I have to tow the line and do whatever is best for us, not be selfish and ask for what I want.

What I realized was that I considered Eddie's needs first, our finances second and my needs last! I only noticed this clearly when the pain of resentment was about to ruin our evening. I had a choice. I could challenge my belief that it was selfish to ask for what I wanted or I could stay stuck in my old pattern. I chose to challenge my thoughts and do a check-in with Eddie.

"Hey, I wouldn't mind getting something different for myself. Maybe something Asian."

He said, "Yeah, Bunny. There's that sushi place around the corner that has line ups all the time. Why don't you try that?"

Wow! He never fails to meet me with kindness and consideration and still my brain wants make him the bad guy. Glad I checked it out. I not only realized he cared about me and not about the money, but I saw how easily my mind makes things up that have no basis in reality at all. It's my past programming coming into play.

Often our thoughts reflect the idea that people are trying to hurt us on purpose. I've discovered that this is rarely true. When I get overcome with emotion because I'm too far afield in Fantasyland, I blow situations out of proportion and create drama out of nothing real.

I blew a gasket one day when I found the usual mess in my car after asking Eddie many times to clean up after he used my car. After calming down, I looked at what I was making the mess in my car mean. It was time for a check in.

"Eddie, when you leave my car in such a mess after asking you over and over not to, I think you are being disrespectful on purpose and that you really don't care about me or my needs."

"You know, I don't even notice that I leave a mess. You know how much I love you. Can you help me find a way to work it out?"

I still don't like it when Eddie leaves my car in a mess, but after this conversation I don't think he's being disrespectful on purpose. I don't make it mean he doesn't care about me. I just get him to clean my car.

A check-in can help you discern whether what you are thinking about a situation is true or whether you are caught up in a destructive fantasy or not. One of the things that spirals us into fantasy thinking is the unfilled parts of our love-o-meter.

CHAPTER 14

Looking For Safety In All The Wrong Places

With mascara running down my face I sat across from my counsellor. She wasn't letting me off the hook by allowing me to make Rod the bad guy. After only a handful of dates, Rod had dumped me and cut me off without a word. I was here to get some relief from my pain.

My counsellor told me that if we don't develop a strong bond with our parents within the first two years of our lives we tend to glom (cling) on quickly to people or things. Without a healthy sense of safety that normally develops with our parents, we cling like needy two-year-olds to our romantic partners.

Light bulb! It's the story of my life.

Visualize this. Your love-o-meter goes to one hundred. The love part is filled up to thirty-five. The other 65% is filled with this sticky, clingy neediness that is really co-dependence. This neediness makes you glom onto the first person who looks like love and safety. So, technically, what feels like love would actually be 35% love and 65% glom. Only by growing the love in your love-o-meter by developing your own sense of inner safety and self-worth will the glom level lower.

It now occurred to me how reaching out to Rod with that sticky, needy glue could not have felt good on his end. It was time for me to learn to love differently.

My counsellor asked, "Do you have friends in your life you know you can count on? Friends that care about you, that would support you if you asked them?"

I listed off a handful of my closest friends. When I thought of my friends, whom I knew wouldn't cut me off or desert me, I felt solid and cared about. I knew they would look after my best interests. It was very different from when I thought about Rod. I didn't feel solid, nor did I feel he cared about me.

She asked, "And how long did it take you to form those friendships and put them in the place they are now?

"Well, years." More light bulbs. I remembered how a relationship is like a child and matures over time. My relationship with Rod was still a tiny baby, whereas my long-time friends were wise and caring adults.

She then said, "I'm going to give you an exercise to do when you get home. Cut out a picture of Cinderella. And then cut out pictures of your friends and paste them around Cinderella. Whenever you start to feel sad or start to pine about Rod, look at Cinderella and imagine what it feels like to be in Fantasyland. Then look at the friends you can count on and sense the difference."

It did make a huge difference. I could clearly feel how unhappy I was when caught by the glommy glue of dependence and then a total sense of relief when I was connected to the solidity of the love in the love-o-meter.

If you grew up in a family where you could have completely open discussions **and** felt very loved, where you were given healthy boundaries while being supported to make your own educated choices, **and** had lots of fun with a family that consistently upheld values that considered everyone, then you had the privilege of growing up in a highly evolved family where your love-o-meter would be quite full, making you feel safe even in the face of adversity. You had a great support system when you needed help.

I have yet to meet a family like this. Some families have aspects of it, yet none are perfect.

Building a sense of safety in life is extremely important. The safer you feel, the calmer you feel and the more you can tune in to your inner guide. If **Lizard Brain** is allowed to kick in all the time, there's no space for love or logic.

Each person has their own version of what feels safe to them. It's important that we figure out what satisfies our own version of this. The more we learn to derive our sense of safety from our own inner resources rather than looking outside ourselves, the more we change our glom (clingy anxiety) to love.

Counselling helped me to nurture my inner sense of safety by learning to ask for my needs to be met. I discovered that it was permissible not only to draw a line in the sand, but to discover where mine is. I learned to develop a support system of friends and family so that I had many resources in times of need and didn't rely on my partner for everything.

When **Lizard Brain** glom kicks in, our perceived safety is threatened so we glom even tighter onto what feels safe or familiar. In our upset, we tend to push our partners away with anger or by shutting down rather than inviting them to share what is going on for us. Once we develop our inner sense of safety and solidity, we know to calm down before saying or doing something regrettable that can damage our partner's trust.

To make it really clear, you know it's glom when you try to control your partner and demand that they behave in a certain way so that you feel comfortable. The communication is conveyed with a tone or an emotion, either overtly or covertly that suggests they are doing something wrong and that your issue is their fault. Being loving, on the other hand, is inviting your partner to participate in meeting your needs with a true open heart, even if you may not like the outcome. There is always free choice for both of you. Following the love portion in your love-o-meter allows you to act with more discernment.

As your sense of safety relies more and more on your inner resources, the temperature of your love-o-meter increases. Once you know how to relate to life from this solid place, you can hear your inner guiding voice that has your best interests in mind instead of **Lizard Brain's** doom and gloom advice.

Leila's relationship with Rob was starting to frustrate her. Rob only spent time with her when he was in emotional distress. He would come over and dump his troubles on her, she would comfort him, they would make love and he would leave. She finally told him, "I'm not willing to have a relationship like this anymore. I want us to have fun together and spend time with each other's friends and families. I would like you to find another means of support for when you're feeling vulnerable because I'm not your counsellor. I want a loving and rewarding relationship for both of us."

Counselling Mind: Leila had been confusing her over-functioning with love. She now sees that her glom had been running the show. She realizes that she would rather love Rob than pity him.

Rob was surprised. He was used to being taken care of by the women in his life and was simply following his family pattern. He had no idea how to be different with women. Rob was open to making a change and agreed to take her on proper dates.

Leila remarks, "It was difficult for both of us at first. I had to learn to draw my own line in the sand and not run to his rescue when he was feeling vulnerable. I had to listen to my heart and not to my glom. He saw that he could have fun with his friends and me at the same time and not compartmentalise his life so much. He suggested he come to counselling with me, as he could see how much it was helping change our relationship. We are now having a lot more fun together."

If the idea of glom is starting to make sense to you, then try this one on.

We've covered the idea that you are in **Cinderella Fantasy** when you see your man as Prince Charming. If he's looking too good to be true then glom is blurring your love lens. On the flip side, when your Prince falls from grace and you think you have finally discovered the "real him" and he's looking like an Ogre, that too comes from the glom portion of your love-o-meter. It's when you try to glom on to your relationship or partner in some way and they don't fulfil your expectation that glom turns into rejection. Without the stable part of your love-o-meter, the back and forth, glom to rejection is how we live in our relationships. Move close, move away, move close, move away.

Be wary when you hear yourself say, "He-can't-do-anything-wrong" or "He-can't-do-anything-right." It means you are doing a glom/rejection dance and it's time to check in with yourself and your partner to find the stable love part of your love-o-meter.

Eddie looked like a total Ogre to me when I thought his eating habits were keeping me away from ordering what I wanted. Only when I got real and checked in with him, did I discover that he wasn't an Ogre at all; in fact, he came up with a suggestion for a great sushi place where I could get exactly what I wanted. Sigh. Love-o-meter goes up a notch.

Most people have a sense of what it feels like to fall in love and have your rosy glasses on. The catch is that this lovely and highly charged state is a normal thing to happen at the start of a relationship, so how do you know it you're perpetually stuck in the fantasy or not? What is your indicator?

It's easy. The women who are not stuck go on to have happy, healthy and productive relationships or marriages. The women who are stuck either have unhappy relationships or can't figure out how to stay in one even though they want to. How do you handle it when you feel your first tinge of disappointment and the fall from grace begins?

As you know, I'm a big fan of counselling and would encourage everyone to get some help, especially if you are caught up in the **Cinderella Fantasy**. I would also encourage everyone to go out and find your spiritual path. Find a way that works for you to be able to tap into your higher power to ask for guidance when you are stuck and then learn to listen for the instruction. For me it comes in the form of knowing in my heart what is right, and I let my inspiration lead me. Sometimes it feels right not to do anything and just wait with curiosity to see what's next. Often I will find the perfect solution to a problem. My job was just to wait patiently and ask for help.

I am a big advocate of transpersonal therapy because it deals with both our spirituality and our humanity. As I was talking about at the end of Chapter 13, it is what helped me take a ride through my own emotional road map so I now have a different relationship to my emotional field. I feel it's the most important journey you can take. Through this style of therapy I have learned to have better relationships with others, which has allowed me to step out of the **Cinderella Fantasy** and open my heart to a caring, committed man who loves me. Most importantly, I have learned to forge a better relationship with myself and with my God so I am led through life with a greater sense of peace, knowing what is really important to me. When my humanity gets in the way of my connection with spirit, I am getting better every day at learning to identify my lack of connection and I know what to do about it when I'm feeling disconnected. I still see a transpersonal counsellor regularly because I feel it's important to continue on this journey with help and a fresh perspective. Just because I now have a relationship, it doesn't mean I've suddenly become perfect at it. I still need a little help now and again.

If you decide to embark on your own journey to love, once you trade your rosy **Cinderella Fantasy** glasses for reality glasses, you see that fantasy behaviour has been colouring everything. The good news is that you can now see all aspects of your life more clearly.

(HAPTER 15

Trading In The Rosy Coloured Glasses

*"The cosmic exchange of gifts within the
greatest Internet in the Universe
is going on all the time. Everyone is wired in;
you just have to receive your mail."*
~ Allen Watson and Robert Perry from the
ACIM Workbook Companion, vol 2.

Anna's Dream

Anna was feeling very angry about the circumstances of her past and was having a good rant at the universe. "God, why has my life been so hard? Why did I have to suffer such abuse as a child? I hate my abusers and I'm angry that I am still affected so many years later. I've had it and I want out of this life!"

Anna's **Lizard Brain** was in high gear.

That night Anna had a vivid dream. "Spiritual guides came and asked me, "So, Anna, how would you have liked your life to be different?"

"I pictured the life I would have liked to have had as a little girl. It was idyllic. I had loving parents and grandparents who showered me with love, affection and all the toys a child could ever want. I had the pet rabbits and the pony I always wanted. I got to play all the time and never had to do chores or help out with the work around the house. I got to have a real childhood with no sexual abuse. It was perfect.

Suddenly I fast-forwarded through the dream to adulthood. I was a self-centred, spoiled woman who tried to control everyone around her. I was used to getting what I wanted without having to lift a finger or contribute in any way. I married a rich man I wasn't in love with. I was an awful, unhappy person.

"When I woke up, I felt like Scrooge on Christmas Day after he met the ghosts of Christmas past. I had been given a new lease on life and felt such an appreciation for all that has taken place and made me who I am. I like who I've become and my life is full and rich. I live in a beautiful place with my husband and kids and I have a career that I find fulfilling. In my dream I got to choose which life I wanted and I chose the one I have. After this experience, I had a much greater trust in why things are the way they are. I realized that my past moulds me in ways I don't realize and the things I thought were bad had an effect on me that I now appreciate. I've learned not to judge any circumstance."

While we may never have a dream or a spiritual awakening like this that allows us to see what goes on behind the scenes of the Universal plan, Anna's dream offers a way of bringing perspective to the life you have. Imagine spending your day in a state of blissful appreciation for the great things in life you do have. Then, imagine spending your day in a state of resentment for the things you wish you had or taking stock of all the ways you've been done wrong. Which day would you choose?

What Kind of a World Do You Live in?

Einstein was asked: "What is the most important question we can ask ourselves?"

He replied, "Is the Universe a friendly place or not?"

In other words, what is the context or the belief structure from which we live our lives?

In Anna's case, she was an abused child so life would have looked particularly scary. The Universe could not have looked friendly to her. Yet, all it took was a dream to completely change her perspective. She went mining for the love in her circumstance to see how it shaped who she had become today, Her life is actually better as she became someone she liked because of her hardships. The circumstances of her life hadn't changed but her outlook had. If we look hard enough we can see our greatest challenges can become our greatest gifts if we take the opportunity to wake up to something new. And that can happen for anyone.

When we are at the mercy of what is outside ourselves, such as someone else's behaviour or some circumstance, the Universe doesn't look a friendly place. When we feel lost, disempowered and angry or upset for any reason, we are identified with our ego. And yet what makes the most sense to me is that we are spiritual as well as human beings and therefore it is our true nature to feel completely joyful, peaceful and alive in every moment.

When the Universe is seen as a friendly place then we feel connected to a larger source, or intelligence field, that supports our fulfilment, peace and happiness. In a friendly

Universe, we know we are loved in every moment and that all is going according to the Universal Plan, even when we are in pain and the plan feels difficult to understand.

It's also important to be able to identify whether it is the ego or the spirit that is whispering in your ear. My human side struggles, plans and fights to find a way to be better or separate from you. When tapped into spirit, nothing else matters except to be loving and open to whatever is unfolding in the moment.

Davidji, a meditation master, describes the difference between our ego and our connected self like this:

> There are two kinds of power that emanate from the self. First is the power of agency, the power that comes from having a famous name, lots of money, or an impressive title. The power of agency can be formidable, but it eventually comes to an end. True power comes from within and it has a spiritual rather than a material foundation. It is permanent and does not die with your body. With agency, indemnity and power come from some external reference, an object, a situation, a status symbol, a relationship, money. With self-power, identity comes from listening to the true self and power comes from the internal reference of spirit. When we take on the power that emanates from that boundless force, nothing is beyond our reach.

To my human, egoic self, I am ready at any moment to protect myself from other people who may hurt me or try to strip me of my power of agency. This defence system creates more pain and a feeling of separateness rather than connection. I need to create a new relationship with my human pain so that I can come to a place of forgiveness and peace. Emotional pain can't be ignored or spiritualized away. Giving my ego-self the attention and nurturing it needs cannot be replaced by jumping to spiritual solutions such as pretending to being grateful or forgiving while still seething inside or feeling righteously superior. Those tactics are like trying to spread icing on a mud cake.

In a friendly Universe, we move through life with a sense of purpose and knowledge that all is well no matter what. We relax into a growing sense of trust, always knowing the best thing to do or say in the moment. We easily love those whom we once felt we needed to protect ourselves from. Now we see them for who they are – people crying out for love rather than people who are intentionally trying to hurt us.

Any counsellor can help you transform a particular problem or difficult relationship in such a way that you can deal with it more effectively. They can help you build your self esteem and feel better about your life and how you interact with the world. With a transpersonal counsellor, you see beyond the struggles of the relationship to how the relationship is the perfect vehicle for clearer connection, giving you the opportunity to move toward your source of inspiration, contentment and joy. Once your perspective is transformed, these feelings permeate everything and the Universe becomes a friendly place. You know you're not alone, that there is a source greater than you that has your best interests at heart and you have greater spiritual resources to draw from.

Personally, I follow *A Course in Miracles* (ACIM) as inspirational reading and practice. There is no particular dogma or doctrine to follow, the premise being that forgiveness of others and myself is the key to finding my own state of happiness. I am learning to trust, especially in times of difficulty, that there is a power greater than myself that I can surrender to and have faith in. Life feels easier. I am now starting to find loving intent in places where I would once only see hurt and pain. I am more content and I can relax, knowing that I am not in charge of the Universal Plan.

One day I finally felt safe enough to throw away my fantasy List and listen to my own heart. I noticed what pulled me towards a man and I learned to heed my heart's cautions. I was able to ask clear and honest questions and observe behaviours that gave me the real information about who I was dating rather than creating another fantasy story.

I know I would never in a million years have answered a profile of Eddie's on a dating site. He would never have fitted any fantasy list that I could have put together. You can write it off to coincidence, but once I stopped "wanting" a relationship and found myself solidly in my happy place, Eddie and I found each other within a couple of months. And now that I know how to find my inner happiness, it makes me a better partner. The inner query continues and keeps my marriage alive as I learn to leave room for both of us to be human and imperfect.

> "Our vulnerabilities are not weaknesses;
> they are powerful reminders to keep our
> hearts and minds open to the reality that
> we're all in this together." ~ Brene Brown

The gold lives in the connection with others. When you are willing to be vulnerable, to admit your part in the divine play and to take an active rather than a reactive stance, you now see any relationship as an opportunity for greater connection with your spiritual source. It requires inner investigation and outer dialogue and outside guidance. I have seen people try to change the way they think on their own and I have never seen it work. You need a fresh perspective to help you see things differently. I encourage you to find a guide for this journey...it is always worth it.

CHAPTER 16

What Happily Ever After Could Look Like

When Eddie came back into my life I was living in a six by eight foot shack called the Dollhouse in the middle of the lawn at Springbrooke retreat centre. I was in the middle of doing a credit proposal, the closest thing to a bankruptcy. So here I was, pushing fifty, living in a tool shed and virtually bankrupt. I considered putting that as the first line on my dating profile. "Old, broke, homeless woman looking for love." Maybe I should also black out a couple of teeth for the full effect. How do you like me now fellas?

Ironically, I don't ever remember feeling happier. I loved my life despite appearing to be what the world would consider "a loser." I loved myself because I didn't make my outer situation mean anything about who I am. I knew I was still inherently lovable and no one could take that away from me.

And then along comes Eddie.

Never having been homeless and broke before, I wasn't sure what the dating protocol would be. When do I say something about my situation? Do I put it on a resume and email it to him? What do I do?

I let it rest until the moment seemed to dictate it. We got together a couple of times, just hanging out, catching up and getting to know one another again. It didn't seem appropriate to share my situation. When I started to sense we were getting closer and had agreed we were going to pursue a relationship, I knew I had to drop the bomb. My hands were shaking. I could feel my heart pounding and sweat beaded on my brow. I looked down at the ground and my voice cracked as the first words struggled to find form. "I have something really important that I have to tell you. I will be really disappointed if you decide to walk away after what I'm about to say, but I completely understand if you do."

The words felt like poison as they spewed out of my mouth and hung in the air. I thought I was going to faint as I waited for the axe to fall. Seconds felt like hours. My fate was now in the hands of the Universe.

Like the rumble of thunder announcing my final judgement, Eddie said, "It doesn't matter. Whatever happens, I think we can get through anything."

The clouds parted and the angels sang. "What?" I squeaked out. I was so stunned I had to ask him to tell me one more time.

"I said it doesn't matter," he repeated tenderly.

And this, dear friends, is why I choose to live with a lime green plastic covered couch and eccentricities too numerous to mention. As paranoid as Eddie is about bed bugs, he is the biggest love bug I know. He melts me. After a year we bought a brand new apartment where there will definitely be no bed bugs and the plastic covered couch ain't coming along.

Above all else what I wish for each of you and the biggest reason that inspired me to write this book was the desire for more people to come to the world of peace, of loving connection, of vulnerability, and of openness.

For over forty years I'd lived in the other world, the one of defence, pride, one-upmanship, better than, guarded safety and of hard and fast opinions, especially those about your life. It's lonely. No one really gets in, not even me.

Lizard Brain feels relieved. He says, "I much prefer sitting in my recliner in the sun than always having to be on high alert. I hate to keep knocking the drinks off the arm of my chair when I leap up to run away. The more women learn to create a sense of solidity and safety for themselves, the more my butt can stay planted firmly in my lounger."

Where do you start? I don't know all the answers for you. I've made a few suggestions based on my own journey, but your path is uniquely yours. However, I guarantee that if you stay curious and open and keep asking questions, your answers will come.

> *"Out beyond ideas of wrong doing and right*
> *doing there is a field.*
> *I'll meet you there."* ~ Rumi

RESOURCES

My favorites

Of course, my own website, www.thelimegreenplasticcov-erecouch.com. You will find free resources there, blogs and videos. Watch for more resources as I build my company. I am starting a talk radio show on www.blogtalkradio.com with my best friend and fellow counsellor, Liz Coleman. We are called The LOVE Therapists. I am going to start a book club of books I read that I think will be helpful for those looking to find love or greater spirituality in their lives.

The rest, dear friends, will reveal itself as the Universe dictates and when I hear it is what you, the readers want the most.

Clearmind International. If you do nothing else, please check out www.clearmind.com. I have never experienced any other personal development psychology that has such a huge and lasting effect in people's lives. On a personal level, they don't claim to make your problems go away, but what they do can help you to deal with your problems in a much more effec-tive way. And then, on a level that will completely bake your noodle, they introduce you to a spiritual connection that has shown me a path to love in a way I never knew existed and to a life of purpose and fulfilment that is beyond words.

A Course in Miracles. www.acim.org Before I did Clearmind's Practitioner's Training course, I looked at this book and my eyes crossed. It made no sense to me. Now, not only do I get it, I think it's one of the best books I have ever read. If you want an easy way to start, do the lessons, or read the book one paragraph at a time and remain curious as to the meaning. It will come.

Allen Watson and Robert Perry www.circleofa.org These two have written several books based on ACIM. If you want something that can translate the ACIM to a language you can understand, these are your guys.

Davidji. www.davidji.com If you want to learn to meditate, Davidji's Guided Meditation CD is a perfect way to start. He does some great teaching and talks you through the meditations so that you can easily follow. If you sign up for his newsletter, he sends out a free meditation every Friday. I like him as he speaks my language. Although he tells you the Sanskrit names of things, he uses practical language I can understand to give direction and I find it very easy.

The Chopra Centre. www.chopra.com. If you have not yet done a free Chopra Centre meditation challenge, please sign up for one. He does a 21 day series every season. They are short and simple and a great introduction to meditation.

Helpful Books

Marianne Williamson www.mariannewilliamson.com She is a huge advocate for ACIM and writes books based on the spiritual nature of the course. Start with A Return to Love.

Anita Moorjani-<u>Dying to be Me</u>-I have been on a kick lately about reading books on near death experience and this is one of my favorites. Most people come back with a complete change in values; the most important being loving kindness.

Geneen Roth-www.geneenroth.com Read <u>Women Food and God</u>. This is a fantastic book. You can substitute the word relationship for every time she uses the word food and you will get a lot out of this. She cuts to the chase in a way that gets past everything to the essence of love in a heartbeat.

<u>Attached</u> www.attachedthebook.com. Although I don't agree with absolutely everything they say in this book, there is some real gold in here if relationships are your hard place.

Candace Pert www.candacepert.com Candace is a ground breaking scientist that not only exposes the culture of the scientific community, more importantly, she bridges the gap between mind and body and science and spirituality. Read anything she writes, but start with <u>Molecules of Emotion</u>

Brene Brown www.brenebrown.com. She is an amazing author and speaker. Check her out on TED TV. Then buy all of her books.

Colin Tipping www.colintipping.com. His book, <u>Radical Forgiveness</u> offers a process that changes your life from hurt, anger and resentment to forgiveness. One you get a small piece of the peace and joy that forgiveness offers your life, you will want more. It's the key to the kingdom.

Byron Katie www.byronkatie.com. Her book, <u>Loving What Is</u> also offers a process to help change your perspective and offer forgiveness. Find which one works best for you.

Movies to Learn From

He's Just Not that into you. My husband Eddie loves this movie and thinks every woman should watch it. If you give your heart too easily to a man, this is a perfect movie.

The Ugly Truth. A cute little romantic comedy of a movie where Katherine Heigl does the perfect dance of turning herself into a pretzel for the guy she thinks she wants. And then she gets caught up in the real unpredictability of love. Put your flannel jammies on, make some popcorn and snuggle up on the couch for the night.

Mark Gungor- www.markgungor.com Watch a Tale of 2 brains. Not only is Mark's presentation hilarious, but you will learn a lot about how to relate to a man with much more success.

What the Bleep. A mind bender. That's all I have to say about that.

Other stuff

Bowen's Family system Theory. www.thebowencentre.org. If you want to learn more about yourself and why you are emotionally built the way you are, this is a great resource. The website is great.

Abraham Hicks. www.abrahamhicks.com. I can't even explain this. I encourage you to just check it out and see if it appeals. I get their daily inspirational emails and many of them have been very helpful.

ABOUT THE AUTHOR

Marion Baker is a Registered Therapeutic Counsellor with a speciality in transpersonal therapy – a modality that marries spirituality and psychology. It took Marion thirty years of searching for love to finally uncover the key to sustaining long-term, loving relationships. Equipped with another way to look at relationships that make them more effective as well as create greater spiritual connection and freedom, she felt compelled to share this ground-breaking perspective with women who have been frustrated in finding lasting love. She resides in Surrey, British Columbia.